C0-AWM-609

MUSIC

for the Academically Talented Student in the Secondary School

WILLIAM C. HARTSHORN

Supervisor in Charge
Music Education
Los Angeles City Board of
Education
Los Angeles, California

Editing Committee:
WILLIAM C. HARTSHORN
WILEY L. HOUSEWRIGHT
ELEANOR TIPTON

National Education Association Project on the Academically Talented Student and Music Educators National Conference, a Department of the National Education Association

1201 Sixteenth Street, N.W.
Washington 6, D. C.

Copyright 1960

NATIONAL EDUCATION ASSOCIATION OF THE UNITED STATES

Library of Congress Catalogue No. 60-53308

Any views expressed or recommendations
implied in this publication do not necessarily constitute official policy of the
Carnegie Corporation of New York, the
Music Educators National Conference,
or the National Education Association.

MT
I
. H 25

Single copy, $1.50. Discounts on quantity orders:
10 percent on 2-9 copies and 20 percent on 10
or more copies. All orders which amount to
$2 or less must be accompanied by funds in pay-
ment. Postage will be added to bills for orders
not accompanied by funds. Copies may be or-
dered from the Music Educators National Conference or the National Education Association,
1201 Sixteenth Street, N.W., Washington, D. C.

CONTENTS

Alma College Library
Alma, Michigan

FOREWORD

Meeting under the joint sponsorship of the Music Educators National Conference and the National Education Association Project on the Academically Talented Student, a group of outstanding music educators spent two and a half days in critical examination of the music curriculum in the secondary schools. Specifically, they considered the problem of identifying, from the literature of music, those experiences which would provide understanding and appreciation in breadth and depth, experiences of a quality to stretch the minds and emotional range of more students, particularly those whom we think of as academically talented but who may or may not have aptitude or interest in performance. The conferees concluded early in their deliberations that if music appreciation was to serve its full measure of purpose, it must take the student into greater depths of understanding of form and style and of interrelationships with other art forms. It should in no sense be a "minor" subject in his program.

In this publication William Hartshorn, working with a committee consisting of Eleanor Tipton and the conference chairman—and with the very helpful and pertinent suggestions of each conference member—has suggested course content and developed a "guide for teaching" which, it is hoped, will make a significant contribution to secondary-school music education, particularly for the academically talented student as distinguished from the musically talented student. The musically talented student is indeed fortunate, for because of his talent he comes to know music as a means of communication. It is the premise of this publication, however, that the lives of other students, too, can be made richer through an understanding of good music.

With the aid of a grant from the Carnegie Corporation of New York, this publication will be made available to school administrators and music teachers throughout the United States. By the implementation of whatever recommended practices are found to be appropriate for a particular school, it is believed that greater meaning can be given to the teaching of music not only for the academically talented student but for all students and thus to the music curriculum and to the life of both the school and the community which it serves.

Special appreciation is due Marcus Hahn for his contribution to Chapter VII and to Karl D. Ernst for his contribution to Chapter X.

WILEY L. HOUSEWRIGHT, Chairman
Conference on Music for the
Academically Talented Student

CHARLES E. BISH, Director
Project on the Academically
Talented Student

THE TOTAL PROJECT

BACKGROUND

THIS PROJECT, sponsored by the National Education Association and aided by a substantial grant from the Carnegie Corporation of New York, involves a number of studies and conferences dealing with the academically talented. A series of volumes devoted to the identification and education of the academically talented student in the American secondary schools will be published as a result of these activities. All major areas of the secondary curriculum will be included. Literally hundreds of administrators and teachers from all parts of the country are participating in one way or another. At the first meeting, in February 1958, approximately 200 outstanding educators and laymen, highly knowledgeable with regard to the above-average boy and girl, met for a few days under the general chairmanship of Dr. James B. Conant.

The work of this large group resulted in a publication of about 160 pages, entitled *The Identification and Education of the Academically Talented Student in the American Secondary School.* With respect to *identification* of the academically talented, the publication discusses methods of identification, measurement and prediction tests of academic ability, and their use. With regard to the *education* of the academically talented, the publication deals with related social and cultural attitudes, motivation, guidance, acceleration, special grouping, and other perennial topics of educational discussion. It then deals briefly with curriculum in English, mathematics, modern language, science, and social studies.

Subsequently, several committees, representing administration and various subject fields in the secondary curriculum, prepared publications that suggest principles, programs, procedures, and course content for the academically talented, in their respective areas.

The present publication is intended to be a counterpart of the others and will take its appropriate place as a part of the total project. It is hoped that readers will find in it some suggestions that will be helpful in strengthening existing programs and in developing additional opportunities in music education for students who are academically talented.

The definition of the academically talented used throughout the project is, of course, a controlling concept in the preparation of this publication. It is recognized that many academically talented students attending our secondary schools are also talented musically. Moreover, it is felt that primary attention to the musical education of the academically talented need not preclude some consideration of highly gifted students who, apart from their intellectual ability, give evidence of extraordinary talent in music. In fact, the types of learnings herein suggested for academically talented students are considered to be equally important for those who possess musical talent of a high order.

Since a program of music education geared to meet the special requirements of academically talented students cannot be separate from the total curriculum, of which music is a part, the types of learnings recommended for academically talented students should bring added substance to existing programs.

THE ACADEMICALLY TALENTED STUDENT

He is one of the million and a half intellectually able young people who are in the upper 15 to 20 percent of secondary-school students in the United States. This does not mean that the academically talented student is to be found in the upper 15 to 20 percent of each individual school. In one school this 15 to 20 percent may mean the upper 1 or 2 percent. In another, it may mean 30 to 40 percent. The academically talented student is to be distinguished from the "gifted" student, who is among the upper 2 percent, computed on a similarly broad basis.

9

HOW HE IS RECOGNIZED

The parent publication of this project points out that tests, whether labeled "intelligence," "aptitude," or "ability," do not measure all of the dimensions of academic talent, but what they do measure seems clearly and consistently related to potentialities for academic achievement. In the chapter by Henry Chauncey, President of the Educational Testing Service, he writes: "If we are searching for sizable intellectual talent, standardized testing will not single out the species or net the catch for us. But it will tell us which pools are likely to contain the 'big ones'." [1]

School marks are another evidence of intellectual ability, but they are not always reliable. A pupil of moderate potential may achieve high marks through persistence while another of exceptional intellectual potentiality may receive marks that give no indication of his true capacity. In the latter case, poor motivation or some maladjustment are but two of the many possible reasons why an academically talented student may be a "low achiever."

The observations of teachers with regard to academic potentiality and personal characteristics can also be helpful in identifying academically talented students, but studies indicate that these observations are likely to be less reliable than standardized tests.

It is probable that a combination of standardized tests, school marks, and teachers' observations can identify academically talented students more accurately than any one of the three functioning alone.

Behavior characteristics of superior and talented or potentially superior and talented students have fre-

---

[1] Chauncey, Henry. "Measurement and Prediction—Tests of Academic Ability." *The Identification and Education of the Academically Talented Student in the American Secondary School.* Report of the Invitational Conference on the Academically Talented Secondary School Pupil. Washington, D. C.: National Education Association, 1958. p. 30.

10

quently been cited. According to one source, such individuals possess the following qualities:

1. A high degree of sensitivity and an inner urge to explore their world—a world which may or may not be acceptable to all elements of society, but within which the individual will quickly develop new understandings, new modes of behavior, and an increasing awareness of environmental factors
2. A high degree of curiosity about the arts, the sciences, and the humanities, as they relate to their environment
3. A capacity for being challenged rather than frustrated by difficulties; a tendency to regard difficulties as steppingstones rather than as insurmountable walls
4. A capacity for identifying and clarifying problematic situations; a capacity for going quickly to the heart of the situation, even though persistent research or continued effort may be required to remove blocks
5. The ability to use hypotheses as tools in the search for solutions; the ability to draw upon past experiences or related endeavors in the formulation of courses of action
6. The ability to act in critical situations; the habit of rejecting conclusions based on prejudice
7. The ability to grasp new insights, profit by new concepts, and develop new generalizations
8. A high sense of intellectual integrity [2]

Others have mentioned the following additional characteristics:

9. The ability to learn as much as other students in less time

---

[2] Kough, Jack. *Practical Programs for the Gifted.* Chicago: Science Research Associates, 1960. 192 p.

10. The achievement of greater precision and accuracy than others
11. The ability to acquire, retain, and understand a greater body of knowledge of greater significance than would be expected of most students.[3]

HIS UNIQUE IMPORTANCE

In a recent publication of the National Education Association, there appeared the following statement concerning the education of the academically talented student:

> Fully capable of becoming a highly accomplished adult and possessing the necessary ability to pursue advanced education in some specialized area, the academically talented student requires an educational program that will enable him to become:
>> A high-level producer in his culture, making a contribution commensurate with his ability in at least one area of specialized endeavor;
>> A high-level consumer, broadly appreciating the riches of contemporary and past achievement, fully aware of the social world in which he lives.[4]

The academically talented student, who may or may not have special gifts in the arts, is likely to be a leader in the society of tomorrow, just as the present leaders in the business, political, and professional life of our country were the academically talented of a generation ago. Some of these exceptional young people may become leaders in scientific or governmental affairs that could significantly change civilization. It is of the utmost importance that they be able to find in music or

---

[3] *Ibid.*

[4] National Education Association, Project on the Academically Talented. *Finding and Educating the Academically Talented Student in the Secondary School.* Report of the Invitational Conference on the Academically Talented Secondary School Pupil. Washington, D. C.: the Association, 1958. p. 8.

in some other fine art a source of beneficence that will strengthen spiritual values in their lives. Some of these leaders in science and government, as well as others among academically talented students, may become members of the boards of directors of symphony orchestras, opera companies, chamber music societies, and art museums. They may serve on committees that determine policies for a public library. They may serve as school administrators, as members of boards of education, or hold any of a variety of other positions that can have an influence in determining the cultural climate of a community. They may be expected to bring to these agencies, so important in our society, the benefits that accrue from the logical thinking of their superior intellects. It is equally to be hoped that their decisions can and will be made out of direct and educative experiences with the arts, rather than out of ignorance of them.

The academically talented student of today is perhaps the richest resource of our nation. It is of the utmost importance to provide the best minds with the best possible education—an education that is broader and deeper than that provided for most students. It has been said, "There is nothing so unequal as the equal treatment of youth of unequal ability." [5]

[5] Scheiflele, Marian. *The Gifted Child in the Regular Classroom.* New York: Teachers College, Columbia University, 1953. p. 44.

II

PURPOSES OF MUSIC EDUCATION FOR THE ACADEMICALLY TALENTED

The academically talented student is first of all a human being, who, by nature, responds to music at the level of feeling and emotion in the same way that other human beings do. It therefore follows that the most basic appeal of music is no different for him than it is for anyone else.

His special intellectual abilities, however, make it possible for him to develop deep insights into the nature and meaning of music as an art. By comparison with the average pupil, he is capable of responding to more mature musical meanings and of understanding more quickly and more completely the form through which these meanings are conveyed. He is capable of a high level of response to musical experiences that are both emotionally compelling and intellectually challenging.

The academically talented student possesses the intellectual capacity to penetrate the complexities of music. Thus, he is able to hear more in a piece of music than other people can, and, hearing more in it, he has a more complete aural concept to which to respond.

If he has ability as a performer, he has the potentiality of adding to the technical and emotional aspects of his performance an intellectual understanding which will convey the formal design and, therefore, the inner meaning of music more clearly to the listener. This potentiality must be matched by the quality of the educational opportunity provided for him.

His musical experiences in the elementary schools may have been of a high, mediocre, or poor quality, or virtually nonexistent. He may have developed real interest in music; or, perhaps, an antipathy to it. He may have learned how to sing or to play an instrument well enough to participate in selective performing groups; or he may have had no opportunity to discover this ability. He may have found that listening to music provides his best contact with it, and he may have learned how to listen with acuity and with genuine

15

sensitivity to musical meanings and values; or he may have had virtually no opportunity to come into contact with the literature of music through listening.

Whether his experiences have been broad and deep or narrow and shallow, he is a human being, and, therefore, the odds are overwhelming that he is naturally responsive to music. But he is also academically talented, and this indicates that his potential responsiveness is of a depth and quality significantly beyond that to be expected of the average student. Thus, he presents a challenge to his teachers to motivate and to guide his activities to the level of achievement of which he, uniquely, is capable.

THE ROLE OF MUSIC IN HIS LIFE

The arts are so significant a part of the cultural heritage of our society that if this heritage is to be passed on to succeeding generations, the educational curriculum must include them. At the present time, the academically talented student is under great pressure for achievement in academic learning. However, if there is to be any balance in his present activities as a student and in his future life as an adult, he must have experiences in the fine arts.

While acknowledging the desirable relaxation from tensions that music and the other arts can provide, it should be recognized that their disciplines are no less exacting than those of any other field of learning. Indeed, the arts are a major discipline and have been so recognized by discerning minds throughout the history of civilization.

Scientists at Los Alamos, who follow a rigorous schedule of tremendously important scientific activities by day, find relaxation by forming string quartets and playing with their colleagues in the evening. Orchestras in various parts of the country, in which participation is

16

limited to members of the medical profession, provide doctors and nurses with mental and emotional release from the accumulated tensions inevitable in their profession. Unquestionably, however, part of the value of these activities for men of science and of medicine is derived from the concentration and mental and physical discipline necessary to perform music in a satisfying manner. Albert Einstein, finding this to be true, was an avid participant in chamber music ensembles.

Music is respected, as well as enjoyed, by academically talented adults because it is more than a casual recreational pleasure. In like manner, a program of music education will appeal to the academically talented student not merely in terms of the pleasures it provides, but, more importantly, because of its musical and educational value. Music will take its proper place in the life of the academically talented student when his musical experiences in school have won his enthusiasm and respect because they have been both a joy to his heart and a challenge to his mind.

SPECIFIC PURPOSES

Fundamentally, the purposes of a program of music education for the academically talented student are not different, in kind, from those for other students. They must be different, however, in breadth and in depth if the potentialities of the academically talented are to be challenged and developed.

The distinguishing purpose of music education for the academically talented, therefore, is to provide, motivate, and guide their musical experiences, both in and out of school, in such a way that these students will greatly exceed other students in the following ways:

1. Their knowledge of facts will be more extensive.
2. Their understandings of relationships among facts will be clearer.

3. Their ability to recognize and understand form *in* music (design) will be increased.
4. Their insights into meanings will be deeper.
5. Their skill in performing and/or in listening will be more advanced.
6. Their performance will be more accurate and precise.
7. Their tastes will be determined less by the whim of the moment than by discriminating judgments of value.
8. Their initiative and independent activity will be stimulated.

The controlling purposes of music education for the academically talented student should be to develop ever-deepening insights into the nature and meaning of music and into the unique way in which music communicates its meaning, and a growing responsiveness, both emotional and intellectual, to that meaning.

More specifically, some of the desirable outcomes of the program, basic to achieving these goals, are as follows:

1. A growing familiarity with important music of all periods and styles, including contemporary music (This should include knowledge of its musical content.)
2. An increasing understanding of the interior design of music (form *in* music) which results from the interrelationships between its constituent elements
3. A knowledge of the stylistic characteristics which distinguish the music of one period from that of another and the ability to recognize them when heard
4. An understanding of the development of the orchestra and its instruments

5. A knowledge of the most significant characteristics of such forms *of* music as symphony, concerto grosso, concerto, opera, cantata, mass, art song, folk song and various types of chamber music

6. An understanding of the role of music as a medium of communication throughout the history of civilization and of how music communicates

7. An understanding of the function of music in contemporary life

8. A knowledge of the scientific and mathematical bases of music

9. A knowledge of authentic relationships that exist between certain important musical compositions and significant works of art or literature

10. The ability to find meanings in music which will enhance understandings in other subject fields

11. A growing realization that music is expressive of intrinsic values and an increasing self-identification with both music and those values

12. An appreciation of the values that are to be found in folk music and the ability to distinguish them from those in the great masterpieces of musical literature

13. An ever-increasing ability to recognize and understand attitudes and values reflected in the music of our country and in the music of other nations (The musical idiom used in our Western civilization is not the only one which has validity.)

14. A growing recognition of the values which distinguish truly artistic and educative music from music which is merely entertaining

15. A growing ability and readiness to distinguish between the personal taste of an individual (himself or another) and the merit of a musical com-

position which may or may not coincide with that taste (This involves the recognition that an individual's taste or distaste for a piece of music makes it neither better nor worse as music.)

16. A growing ability to distinguish between fiction about musicians and factual biographies—to recognize authenticity in what is read

17. An increasing knowledge of the titles and authors of definitive works on musical subjects and awareness of the importance of these works as sources of reference.

III

A MUSIC
CURRICULUM FOR THE
ACADEMICALLY TALENTED

Since the over-all purpose of music education for academically talented students is their musical growth, and since the essential characteristic of growth is continuity, the curriculum should provide for a continuity of musical experience which will promote the progressive development of understandings, insights, judgments, and skills. A program which does not provide academically talented students with such a continuity of experience deprives the best minds of the quality of music education they deserve.

The purposes and activities suggested in this publication cannot be considered to be separate from the total instructional program of the school. Indeed, they should take their place as a significant part of the school's curriculum, and, as these opportunities are made available both to academically talented and musically talented students, the result should be a strengthening of the over-all existing program.

In some situations, the purposes, activities, and content suggested for academically talented students may constitute the basis for scheduling a particular course for them. The intent, however, is not so much to recommend the organization of a specialized course in music for academically talented students as to indicate the types of learning most appropriate to them. These kinds of learning may involve one course or several; a course organized primarily for performance and which also provides for other musical activities; a course organized primarily around listening activities and which also includes some performance, as well as related reading, analysis, and discussion; or individual or small group activities outside of any organized class structure. The situation in which the learning takes place is, from the point of view of this publication, less important than the scope, depth, and quality of the learning itself.

It is to be expected that the special characteristics of academically talented students (curiosity, imagination, initiative, and self-propelled desire to learn) will lead them to explore areas of learning related to, but outside of, the scope of the course in which they are enrolled. Obviously, such activity should receive strong encouragement, including provision of necessary source materials and student presentations to the class of the results of particular studies undertaken. It is also desirable that the total resources of the music department be made available to academically talented students, e.g., a student in a performing group may desire the assistance of a teacher of theory or of music history. The academically talented student should be given every opportunity to move at will across the boundaries that separate the various subjects in the music curriculum.

BROAD TYPES OF ACTIVITY

The activities through which the academically talented student grows musically will differ from those of most students, chiefly in the extent to which they are characterized by a greater degree of intellectual involvement and self-initiated, self-directed performance, listening, research, and creative activity.

For the academically talented student whose previous experiences have included a high level of vocal or instrumental performance, or both, it is important that this performance be continued with uncompromising adherence to the highest standards of repertoire and technical proficiency. It is essential, however, that ample provision also be made for listening, analysis, reading, writing, and discussion, so that he can grow in understanding the meaning of the music he performs, as well as of other music. Skills alone are not enough for the academically talented student.

There may be some academically talented students for whom performance has become an activity of minor importance and, perhaps, one in which they have had only moderate success. These students need not abandon performance altogether, but their activities should involve a greater emphasis upon listening and related studies that are intellectually oriented.

For one reason or another, large numbers of academically talented students may have no desire to perform music with any serious intent. For this group, the curriculum should provide musical experiences that consist chiefly of listening, analyzing, reading, and reacting to these experiences through writing or discussion. These opportunities should result in a high level of enjoyment, involving responses that are both emotional and intellectual. They should also lead to deep understandings and insights, and to discriminating judgments of value.

For these three groups of academically talented students, the program will vary chiefly in the relative emphasis placed upon performance, for the other activities are essential in all cases if these exceptional young people are to be musically educated.

Academically talented students may wish to relate learnings from other subject fields to their musical activities. This is desirable and to be encouraged, provided a direct and authentic relationship exists, and provided that it strengthens learning in the field of music.

SPECIFIC ACTIVITIES

The specific purposes and activities suggested in this publication are not intended to be inclusive. They are, in fact, merely suggestive of types of learnings and activities that should characterize the musical education of the academically talented. The diversity of interests to be expected from the inquiring minds of a group of academically talented students is so great that it would be impossible to include all of the possibilities, or even to anticipate them.

In addition to the regular activities which occupy most students of music, it is suggested that academically

24

talented students (for whom these are appropriate) take part in the following activities:

- Participate in seminars, honors courses, small study groups, or performing organizations which may meet during the school day, in the school but after school hours, or which are organized by community agencies
- Attend rehearsals of professional groups and concerts presented in the community
- Make contact with important professional musicians and interview them
- Interview a local concert manager for the purpose of investigating and reporting his function and his problems
- Interview religious leaders of various faiths as a method of investigating the nature and function of the music used in their services
- Interview the head of a radio or television station or an advertising agency to discover reasons for the use of singing commercials
- Investigate and report on the music of ethnic groups prominent in the community, with special attention to the ways in which they use music and the melodic, rhythmic, and harmonic idioms employed
- Become familiar with the facilities of the music department of the public library and learn how to use them
- Read responsible criticisms and magazine articles which deal with significant musical developments and personalities
- Compare the letters of composers with their biographies, relating the material, as much as possible, to music that can be heard or performed
- Take advantage of every opportunity to listen with careful attention to serious music provided by mass media of communication

- Prepare program notes for the presentation of a recording to the class (as though the music were being performed at a concert)
- Write the program notes for concerts given by performing groups in the school (Research will be necessary to ensure their authenticity.)
- Write an obituary notice that might have been printed in a Vienna newspaper on the day following Beethoven's death. Follow this by writing an article which might be printed in the same newspaper in 1970 to celebrate the 200th anniversary of his birth, placing him in proper perspective in so far as his life and his works are concerned
- Write a review of a concert, discussing both the music and its performance
- Write a review comparing two recordings of the same composition
- Prepare a paper showing how the development of instruments has affected the writing of major composers. In preparing it, numerous recordings, musically illustrative of the topic, should be heard. Study the scores of these compositions and read authentic information about them. A specific area for this activity might be a comparison of the writing for the French horn by Mozart and by Richard Strauss.
- Write an essay relating the *Symphonie fantastique* by Berlioz to the symphonies which preceded it. Indicate its influence upon the music of Wagner, Liszt, and Richard Strauss. (This can be of great value if it grows out of experience with the music itself. It will be of little value if it is developed through reading which is apart from the music.)
- Prepare a tape recording of a documentary account of the life of some composer, including performance of some of his music by other students or from recordings.

26

In making a report concerning an opera, the average student is likely to be content with discussing very little more than the plot and, to some extent, the music. The academically talented, however, are likely to consider its psychological, allegorical, philosophical, or social significance. They will be interested in exploring other areas of learning related in some way to music which they may have heard. The possibilities of such exploration may motivate the study of a particular composition.

The following, while in no way inclusive, are suggestive of areas for related independent study:

- For the academically talented student who is interested in American poetry—A comparison of Edward Arlington Robinson's poem, *Tristram*, with Wagner's *Tristan und Isolde* (including reading of the libretto). After he has heard the music, a study of the writings of Lawrence Gilman [1] and Ernest Newman [2] will help him to understand better both Robinson's poem and Wagner's music

- For the academically talented student who is interested in tragedy in literature—A study of Verdi's *Macbeth*, both as music and in relation to Shakespeare's drama. A further comparative study of these two works, in relation to the psychological, emotional, and physical disintegration of Boris Godunov (Pushkin's poem and Mussorgsky's opera), would be a significant area of independent research, provided it is based upon direct experience with the music

- For the academically talented student who is interested in social studies—A study of Gluck's *Orfeo ed Euridice*, considering its allegorical expression of

[1] Gilman, Lawrence. *Wagner's Operas*. New York: Farrar and Rinehart, 1937. p. 145-191.

[2] Newman, Ernest. *The Wagner Operas*. New York: Alfred A. Knopf, 1949. p. 169-278.

the necessity for mutual confidence in human affairs

- For the academically talented student who is interested in philosophical concepts—A study of the music of *Also sprach Zarathustra* by Richard Strauss, as related to the passages from Nietzsche to which it unquestionably refers. (The unique characteristics of the section entitled "Of Science" will be of special significance, for it is a fugue in which the subject uses every note in the chromatic scale)

- For the academically talented student who is interested in a study of chivalry or of dramatized conflict between good and evil—A study of Wagner's *Lohengrin,* which can be a significant musical experience related to this particular interest

- For the academically talented student interested in Gregorian chant—A study of *The Third Symphony* by Paul Creston

- For the academically talented student who is interested in the nature of satire and its literary or dramatic expression—A comparative study of Wagner's *Die Meistersinger* and *Ein Heldenleben* by Richard Strauss. This should involve an analysis of the music itself and research into those personal experiences of the composers with their critics which affected the nature of the music. Such a study can lead to the development of important concepts concerning music criticism

- For the academically talented student who is interested in the general topic of heroism and musical expressions of it—A comparative study of *Ein Heldenleben* and the *"Eroica" Symphony* by Beethoven, not only in terms of their contrasting concepts of heroism but in terms of the musical content and style through which these concepts are communicated

- For the academically talented student who is interested in the history of this country—Hearing and studying the *New England Triptych* by William Schuman. This music is based upon compositions of the Revolutionary period written by William Billings. Schuman's treatment of it also provides an opportunity to study contemporary methods of composition and orchestration

- For the academically talented student who is interested in world problems caused by greed and lust for power, and in possible solutions to these problems—An enormously challenging study, of monumental proportions, may be made of *The Ring of the Nibelung* by Richard Wagner. This is a potential subject for independent research and inquiry which might possibly require a matter of months. If the study involves an analysis of the music itself, including its leitmotifs, and if the unfolding of the plot is considered in relation to symbolisms such as those outlined by Lawrence Gilman,[3] Ernest Newman,[4] and Paul Bekker,[5] its rewards can be as great as the magnitude of the project

- For the academically talented student who is interested in Shakespearean drama—A comparative study of music related to the story of Romeo and Juliet, as composed by Berlioz, Tchaikovsky, Prokofiev, and Gounod

- For the academically talented student who is interested in French literature—A comparative study of the music composed by Debussy, Fauré, and Sibelius, in connection with the story of Pelléas and Mélisande.

---

[3] Gilman, Lawrence, *op. cit.,* p. 65-144.

[4] Newman, Ernest, *op. cit.,* p. 393-634.

[5] Bekker, Paul. *Richard Wagner: His Life in His Work.* London: J. M. Dent & Sons, Ltd., 1931. 522 p.

IV

MUSIC AS
A MEANS
OF COMMUNICATION

The following pages are devoted to some fundamental concepts concerning music as a means of communication. These concepts are considered to be important areas of understanding for the academically talented student. The extent to which they have meaning for him will depend entirely on the extent to which they are related to direct experience with music, through either performing or listening. The particular music to be used for this purpose will vary in different localities, at different grade levels, and with different groups of students at the same grade level. It is essential, however, that these concepts be understood in a musical context.

SOME FUNDAMENTAL CONCEPTS

Music has always been an essential means of communication. In the earliest days of civilization, primitive people used music as a language to convey meanings common to the routine affairs of life and also to express feelings, emotions, ideals, and aspirations of special significance to them. Today, people less civilized than we think we are, still use music in the same way.

This was vividly portrayed in the spring of 1960 in a filmed telecast from Nigeria where, at that time, nearly 80 percent of the people could neither read nor write. In this telecast, a drummer demonstrated how he would play a drum to let his fellow citizens know that President Eisenhower was arriving and should be welcomed. Both rhythm and variations in pitch were involved. The same telecast showed music being used to arouse nationalistic fervor in Nigeria. Large numbers of Nigerian young people and adults were seen singing enthusiastically as an expression of their extremely intense desire for national independence and unity. The primitive power of their music was unmistakable.

By contrast, the same telecast used a passage from *A Lincoln Portrait,* by Aaron Copland, as a basic continuity theme. In this context, the use of this highly sophisticated music, which emotionalizes the ideals of Abraham Lincoln, communicated a meaning beyond verbal description.

This telecast was an example of twentieth-century people, some still uneducated and others more civilized, using music to convey meanings involving feelings so intense that only music could express them adequately.

Music has remained a simple folk art, expressive of ordinary experiences in the lives of people. It has also become a highly refined art through which some of the greatest minds in human history have expressed some of the noblest thoughts and loftiest ideals of which human beings are capable. There are values in each of these types of music. It is important to recognize the distinctions between them.

Trivial feelings can be expressed by trivial music. This happens constantly. The higher the level of human experience to be expressed, however, the higher must be the qualitative level of the music to communicate it adequately. We feel most deeply about the things for which we care the most and, consequently, hold in highest value. Our deepest feelings are, therefore, equated with values that give meaning and purpose to our living. Music, as the expression of feeling, thus becomes symbolic and expressive of those values which are intrinsic and are identified with the spiritual nature and aspirations of man. This is thoroughly appropriate, for unlike the visual arts, which deal with material objects that occupy space, the distinguishing characteristic of music is tone, which is not material and does not occupy space, but moves in time.

Academically talented young people are capable of deep understanding of truly great music, including both its emotional and its intellectual aspects. The best young minds of our time deserve contact with the finest thoughts of present and previous generations, many of which are communicated in works of great composers.

WHAT MUSIC COMMUNICATES

Strictly speaking, music communicates only its own content—melody, rhythm, and harmony (tempo, dynamics, and tone color are also part of its content). The key to the meaning of a considerable amount of music is to be found in the melodic, rhythmic, and harmonic interrelationships between one part of a composition and another. For example, one section of a composition may repeat a melodic pattern from an earlier passage but with a different rhythm, or it may repeat a rhythmic pattern with a different melody. This type of relationship is form, not in the gross sense, but as design. It is form *in* music as distinguished from forms *of* music, and is a highly significant part of what is communicated. To repeat, what music communicates is precisely its musical content, including its form.

There is, however, a substantial literature of music in which the composer has indicated, either through the wording of a title or through specific reference to nonmusical ideas, that he intended his music to suggest ideas, scenes, narratives, or other concepts that are not musical.

The academically talented student should have broad experience with music of both types and should recognize that the value of each is to be found in its musical content rather than in any associative idea. For this reason, major attention should be given to the music itself, with other concepts receiving only secondary consideration.

Some examples in this connection are the following:

	Music which is dissociated from extramusical implications	Music inspired by or intended to be suggestive of nonmusical ideas
BACH	Little Fugue in G Minor	Passion According to St. Matthew
HAYDN	Symphony No. 88 in G Major	The Creation
MOZART	Symphony No. 39 in E Flat	The Magic Flute
BEETHOVEN	Symphony No. 2 in D Major	Leonore Overture No. 3
SIBELIUS	Concerto for Violin and Orchestra	The Swan of Tuonela
RAVEL	String Quartet in F Major	Mother Goose Suite
DEBUSSY	String Quartet in G Minor	La Mer
THOMPSON	Symphony No. 2	The Testament of Freedom
BARBER	Symphony No. 1	Medea's Meditation and Dance of Vengeance
COPLAND	Sonata for Violin and Piano	A Lincoln Portrait

Since people differ in what they can hear in a piece of music, the meaning they find in it may differ, too. With increasing experience in listening, a student becomes able to hear more of what is in a piece of music. Thus, it may not have identical meaning for him at two different times. Although the content of a given piece of music is the same today as it will be ten years from now, his understanding of what a composition means will change in the sense that it increases developmentally over a period of time.

HOW MUSIC COMMUNICATES

In music education, more important than *what* music means is *how* it means it, for in developing an understanding of how music communicates, the student is dealing with the content of music itself.

Academically talented students will penetrate more deeply into the "how" of musical communication than will other students; and they will do so with music that is more mature and technically more advanced. For example, in working with average students, it might be appropriate to begin a study of the theme and variation form with Cailliet's clever *Variations on "Pop Goes the Weasel."* Academically talented students, however, are capable of approaching this form through more mature works, such as the *Symphonic Variations* by César Franck or the *Variations on a Theme by Haydn* by Brahms.

If that which is communicated by music is its content, an understanding of how music communicates will be developed by studying its content, with particular reference to the relationships among the constituent elements and the way composers have used this content for expressive purposes. For example, the meaning of Bach's *Little Fugue in G Minor* is communicated by the following:

1. Its melodies, the first of which begins with a three-note pattern that establishes the tonic chord in G minor
2. Its rhythmic content, which consists primarily of two quarter notes and a dotted quarter note followed by a succession of eighth notes, all of them being in $\frac{4}{4}$ meter
3. Its harmony, which, at the beginning, is implicit in the melodic line of the first theme and subsequently results from contrapuntal combinations of melody
4. Its tempo, which, when correct, is appropriate to the sturdy quality of its opening theme; but which, when too fast, reduces the grandeur of this music to something less significant

5. Its dynamics, which gradually develop into a powerful climax because of the increasing number of melodic parts and the increasing dynamic level with which they are performed

6. Its form, which becomes clear to the performer and/or the listener as he recognizes the way in which earlier melodies are imitated by subsequent melodies.

Consider now *The Swan of Tuonela* by Sibelius. Its *musical* meaning, like that of Bach's *Fugue,* is communicated by the nature of its musical content as follows:

1. Its melodies, which are long, gently undulating, and songlike

2. Its harmonies, which are predominantly minor and change with comparative infrequency

3. Its rhythms, which move smoothly even when there are crosscurrents of rhythmic movement (as at letter G in the score)

4. Its tone color, which is decidedly dark due to the following factors:
   The absence of flutes and trumpets
   The somber tone of the English horn, which is the solo instrument
   The use of mutes on the stringed instruments, which are divided into an extraordinary number of parts
   The use of *col legno* in the strings
   The scoring for wind instruments beginning at letter G

5. Its form, in which each phrase in the solo instrument seems to emerge inevitably from the previous one and in which the passage for strings at the end refers back to the beginning of the music

6. Its tempo, which is slow

7. Its dynamics, which rarely reach a *forte.*

This musical content is its musical meaning. The composer, however, gave this composition a title. He also wrote the following lines on the score, "Tuonela, the land of death, the hell of Finnish mythology, is surrounded by a large river with black water and a rapid current, on which the Swan of Tuonela floats majestically, singing." Thus, to the purely musical meaning, Sibelius has added nonmusical ideas to be associated with the composition. It is instructive to relate the two, for Sibelius determined the character of the music in terms of the particular communicative purpose suggested by the above quotation.

It is also desirable for the academically talented student to recognize the importance of tone color in communicating the meaning of vocal music. An example, perhaps somewhat extreme, can be found in Bach's *Passion according to St. Matthew.* The chorus that almost shouts for the release of Barabbas and later shouts to "have Him crucified" obviously uses a completely different color of vocal tone than is used in the final chorus, "Here yet Awhile," which has the effect of a lamentation over the grave of the Crucified One.

Academically talented young people may grow in their understanding of how music communicates as they hear, analyze, and discuss compositions which are sharply contrasting in the nature of their musical content. The following are a few examples suggested for study:

Melody

The smoothly flowing melodic lines of Palestrina's music in contrast to the angularity of some of Stravinsky's melodies

The melodic content of Debussy's *La Mer* contrasted with the *Overture to The Flying Dutchman* by Wagner, or Mendelssohn's overture, *Fingal's Cave*

37

Rhythm

The comparative simplicity of rhythms in the music of C. P. E. Bach as contrasted with the syncopation and cross rhythms in much of the music of Brahms

The comparative simplicity of the rhythms in a Shaker tune such as *Simple Gifts* as contrasted with the variety and complexity of rhythms found in Copland's *Appalachian Spring*. A similar example can be found in *Chester* by William Billings as contrasted with the last movement of William Schuman's *New England Triptych* which is based upon the same melody

Harmony

The essentially diatonic and narrowly restricted harmonic content of *The Christmas Concerto* by Corelli or the "Pastoral Symphony" from Handel's *Messiah* in contrast to the richly colorful and chromatic harmony of another pastoral, *The Afternoon of a Faun* by Debussy

The harmonic texture which results from the interweaving of melodic lines in the *Little Fugue in G Minor* by Bach in contrast to the vertical harmonic quality in that composer's chorale, *Komm Süsser Tod*

The harmonic characteristics of Johann Pachelbel's motet, *Now Thank We All Our God,* as contrasted with the harmony in William Schuman's cantata, *A Free Song*

Form

The compactness and regularity of design in the last movement of Mozart's *Symphony No. 40 in G Minor* as contrasted with the looseness of design in any of the *Hungarian Rhapsodies* by Liszt, noting that the rhapsody is intentionally a "free" form

The comparative simplicity of the variation form in the *24th Caprice* by Paganini as contrasted with the enormously complex treatment of this same theme by Brahms in his *Variations on a Theme by Paganini* and by Rachmaninoff in his *Rhapsody on a Theme of Paganini* (Although both are so-called "free" forms, the contrasts among the three help to clarify an understanding of each.)

The strictness of the formal design in a canon such as is found in the last movement of the *Sonata in A Major for Violin and Piano* by César Franck as contrasted with the comparative freedom of design in Chausson's *Poème for Violin and Orchestra*

Tone Color

The extraordinary variety of tone color in both the voice and the instrument as each is altered in a manner appropriate to the different poems which comprise Benjamin Britten's *Serenade for Tenor, Horn, and Strings*

The piercing, awesome "Wolf's Glen" tone of the clarinet in Weber's *Overture to Der Freischutz* in contrast to the smooth, ingratiating clarinet tone for " 'Twas Brillig and the Slithy Toves" in the Jabberwocky movement of *Through the Looking Glass* by Deems Taylor.

The depth and richness of vocal tone as Isolde sings the closing passage of *Tristan und Isolde* as contrasted with the bloodcurdling sounds of Salome following the beheading of John the Baptist in Strauss' opera which bears her name.

THE PERFORMER

In considering how music communicates, it is impossible to ignore the performer, for, in a sense, music is at the mercy of the performer for its communication. It is important that academically talented young people, who may be determining musical policies in their communities in the future, develop insights into principles of musical performance and become discriminating in evaluating the qualities of a given performance.

In this connection, these young people should develop the ability to follow musical notation, including orchestral scores. They may find it highly instructive to hear two or more recordings of the same work by different performers, while following the score to evaluate the merits of each performance in terms of what the composer wrote. Through this activity they may also develop an understanding of the inherent relationship which must exist between form and tempo. (In a sonata allegro form, for example, if two themes that are heard separately in the exposition section are combined so that they are heard simultaneously in the recapitulation section, this is a matter of form, but it also calls for the two themes to have the same tempo in the exposition section.)

Printed details to be noticed in the score, in addition to the notes, will include indications of initial meter and tempo and subsequent changes thereof, dynamics, phrasing, and indications providing for comparative balance between sections of the orchestra. Every detail is important, not excepting even a seemingly insignificant indication for *staccato*. It should be noted particularly that indications for the music to be louder do not imply that it must at the same time be faster, and, conversely, indications that the music should be softer do not imply that it should be slower. In fact, it is interesting to note that many of the characteristics of the most artistic performances are likely to be the exact opposite of those which seem to be most natural in terms of amateurish tendencies.

It is important, also, to consider the appropriateness of interpretation to the style of the composer. For example, music may be communicating properly if there is *rubato* in a nocturne by Chopin but improperly if there is *rubato* in a fugue by Bach.

THE SPECIAL IMPORTANCE OF FORM IN MUSIC

The ability to recognize one part of a piece of music as having been derived from another part is a key to musical understanding on the part of both the performer and the listener. Such an understanding is indispensable to intelligent performing or listening. This presents the student with a major challenge, for while the other elements of music appeal directly to the senses, form engages the mind. The listener may be aware of melody and rhythm and enjoy them while remaining in a relatively passive state of body and mind. If, however, he is to discover any aspect of the form of the music and begin to understand the interrelationships between the various elements in a composition through which it makes sense with itself, he must give conscious attention to details in the music, remember them with imagery, and exercise creative thought of the sort that discovers relationships between ideas.[1]

It therefore follows that the development of clear understanding of form (in the sense of design) is particularly appropriate to the intellectual capacities of the academically talented student and necessary to intelligent performance by the musically talented. If this aspect of music education is neglected, the program, at best, can be only partially educative.

---

[1] Hartshorn, William C. "The Role of Listening." *Basic Concepts in Music Education.* Fifty-Seventh Yearbook, Part I, National Society for the Study of Education. Chicago: University of Chicago Press, 1958. Chapter 11, p. 263-64.

V

FORMS OF
MUSICAL
COMMUNICATION

In previous discussion, the term *form* has been used in relation to the repetition of phrases or patterns, whether in identical or altered form, through which an inner unity is achieved in a piece of music so that it makes sense with itself. This is form *in* music. Since it is characteristic of the academically talented mind to organize concepts, a study of form in a broader sense— forms *of* music—will appeal to many academically talented students.

FORMS OF MUSIC

Such a study might include simple two- and three-part forms, a rondo form such as A-B-A-C-A, and the sonata allegro form which is characterized by thematic development.

Similar studies may be made in connection with song forms. In this regard, some comparisons are useful. For example, the student may consider the strophic *Heidenröselein* by Schubert in contrast to his "through-composed" *Du bist die Ruh.* In like manner, such simple strophic songs as the *Lullaby* or the *Blacksmith* by Brahms may be contrasted with his great "through-composed" setting of the 13th Chapter of First Corinthians in the *Four Serious Songs,* Opus 121.

Academically talented students should learn the significant and distinguishing characteristics of various *gross forms* of musical communciation, first in direct contact with the music itself through listening or performing, and then through reading about the forms and discussing them. Such forms include:

Theme and Variations	Mass
Sonata	Oratorio
Suite	Opera
Symphony	Overture
Concerto Grosso	Symphonic Poem
Concerto	Chamber Music

For the academically talented student, the theme and variations and the passacaglia can provide significantly educative experiences, for, in each of them, basic thematic material is repeated either in altered form or with variations which move around the theme in its original form. In the theme and variations, the "what" of its communication is identical with the "how" of its communication, for, in almost every case, its purpose is to be found in its form. A possible exception, however, is Elgar's *Enigma Variations* in which he intended each variation to be a musical portrait of someone he knew. In addition to this work, compositions, in the form of theme and variations and passacaglia, appropriate for study by the academically talented include:

Theme and Variations

Movements of the cantata, *Jésu, Priceless Treasure* by Bach
Variations on a Theme by Diabelli by Beethoven
Variations on a Nursery Theme by Dohnanyi
Variations and Fugue on a Theme of Mozart by Max Reger
Variations on a Theme by Haydn by Brahms

Passacaglia

Passacaglia and Fugue in C Minor by Bach
Symphony No. 4 in E Minor by Brahms (final movement)
First Symphony by Samuel Barber (closing section)

Obviously, each of these compositions is a work of emotional appeal and intrinsic worth, but each is mentioned also because of its educative potentialities with respect to form.

Similar learnings may be developed through performing, hearing, and analyzing contrapuntal forms such as the canon and fugue. Contact with the music precedes the analysis. The ability to hear two or more parts si-

44

multaneously, while performing or listening, is basic to musical understanding. Numerous fugues have been mentioned previously. Significant passages in canonic form may be found in the following works:

Canonic Form

Sonata in A Major for Violin and Piano by César Franck (final movement)

"Nocturne" from the *String Quartet in D Major* by Borodin

Symphony in D Minor by César Franck (first and third movements)

Roman Carnival Overture by Berlioz

Variations and Fugue by Weinberger on the melody of "Under the Spreading Chestnut Tree," in which both the theme and its canonic imitation are combined in retrograde (mirror) so that four melodic lines are imitating each other simultaneously

If the academically talented student is to become a broadly educated person, he should have a knowledge of the major forms of music. To know their distinguishing characteristics as a fact, however desirable that may be, is of less significance than to have experienced them directly as a musically communicative medium. Only through such experience will this knowledge have meaning.

The academically talented student should understand that composers communicate their musical ideas through various forms of composition and that the nature of the form is determined by the character of the musical idea to be communicated. There is, therefore, a close relationship between the communicative purpose of the composer and the particular form in which he writes. Each should be studied in relation to the other. Although big forms have sometimes been used to communicate small ideas, the biggest ideas usually require large forms. For example, the *Ninth Symphony*, the *Missa Solemnis* and

45

the last string quartets by Beethoven, *The Ring of the Nibelung* by Wagner, the *Mass in B Minor* by Bach, or Verdi's *Otello* convey concepts of such proportions that only large forms are adequate to express them.

The academically talented student will find it instructive to hear and analyze symphonies in which the three or four movements, characteristic of many works in this form, have been combined into one movement. A study of the *Symphony No. 4 in D Minor* by Schumann will show an intermediate, transitional step in this direction. Notable examples of symphonies in one movement are the *Symphony No. 7 in C Major* by Sibelius and the *Symphony No. 1* by Barber. A study of the content and formal pattern of these symphonies will reveal interesting comparisons with the structure of earlier symphonies that will clarify the understanding of each.

VI

CHARACTERISTICS
OF MUSICAL STYLE

The academically talented student should be able to identify, by ear, baroque (1600-1750), rococo (1725-75), classical (1775-1815), romantic (1825-1900), impressionistic (late nineteenth and early twentieth centuries), and nationalistic (nineteenth century to the present) music. There are certain stylistic overlappings among these periods, but the predominant characteristics should be identified.

This study of characteristics of musical style begins with direct experience with the music itself, through performance or listening. From these activities understandings and insights are developed. Analysis, reading, and discussion clarify the concepts which are first made evident through the music. The academically talented student who successfully engages in this study will have a broader and deeper knowledge upon which to base his judgments concerning various idioms and styles, and the cultures with which they are associated.

An academically talented student who is participating in a comparative study of idioms and styles in musical composition, accompanied by adequate musical illustrations of them, is less likely to permit his emotional reactions to interfere with his intellectual response to music in unfamiliar idioms. The inevitable historic connotations of a comparative study of musical styles will give the academically talented student a perspective of the development of music during the past three centuries—but this is an outcome, not a dominant purpose.

The academically talented student should also be knowledgeable about stylistic characteristics evident in the music of representative contemporary composers, such as Igor Stravinsky, Arnold Schoenberg, Alban Berg, Béla Bartók, Paul Hindemith, Sergei Prokofiev, Dmitri Shostakovich, Ralph Vaughan-Williams, Benjamin Britten, Arthur Honegger, Darius Milhaud, Francis Poulenc, Zoltán Kodály, Heitor Villa-Lobos, Carlos Chavez, Aaron

Copland, Samuel Barber, Paul Creston, Howard Hanson, Walter Piston, and William Schuman.

Continuing consciousness of stylistic characteristics in music that is heard is desirable. It means little merely to memorize verbalizations concerning characteristics of style. The recognition of style as an important factor in the "how" of musical communication is infinitely more important.

SUGGESTED COMPARATIVE STUDIES

Since characteristics of musical style cannot be studied apart from the forms of music through which they become evident, it may be desirable for the academically talented student to make a comparative study of styles within one or more of the forms of music mentioned in the previous section. Among the vast number of possibilities in this connection, a few are suggested here. They are organized according to the form within which contrasting styles may be studied:

Sonata

Sonatas for violin and piano, by J. S. Bach, Mozart, Beethoven, Schubert or Schumann, Dvôrák, Debussy, Hindemith, and Copland

Suite

Suites for orchestra by J. S. Bach
Serenades by Mozart
Suites, by Tchaikovsky, Richard Strauss, Debussy or Ravel
Facade by Walton
Mikrokosmos Suite for Orchestra by Bartók
Air Power by Dello Joio

Mass

Missa Papae Marcelli by Palestrina
Mass for Four Voices by Byrd
Mass in C, K. 427 (The Great) by Mozart

Mass in G by Schubert
Missa Choralis by Liszt
Mass (1948) by Stravinsky

Oratorio

Belshazzar by Handel
The Creation by Haydn
Elijah by Mendelssohn
Belshazzar's Feast by Walton
Mass of Life by Delius

Opera

Orfeo ed Euridice by Gluck
Magic Flute by Mozart
Die Meistersinger by Wagner
Salome by Richard Strauss
Falstaff by Verdi
Boris Godunov by Mussorgsky
Pelléas et Mélisande by Debussy
Rake's Progress by Stravinsky

Concerto Grosso

Works entitled *Concerto Grosso,* by Handel, Bloch, and Stravinsky

Concerto

Concertos for piano (or harpsichord) and orchestra or for violin and orchestra, by J. S. Bach, Mozart, Beethoven, Brahms, Dvôrák, and Prokofiev

The *Concerto for Orchestra* by Vivaldi and by Bartók

Chamber Music

String quartets, by Mozart or Haydn, Beethoven, Smetana, Debussy or Ravel, Schoenberg, Bartók, Barber, Mennin

Quintets for piano and winds, by Mozart, Beethoven, Rimsky-Korsakov.

Symphony

Symphony No. 88 in G Major by Haydn
Symphony No. 3 in E Flat ("Eroica") by Beethoven
or
Symphony No. 6 in F ("Pastorale") by Beethoven
Symphonie Fantastique by Berlioz
Symphony No. 1 in B Flat ("Spring") by Schumann
Symphony No. 1 in C Minor by Brahms
Symphony in D Minor by Franck
Symphony No. 2 ("London") by Vaughan-Williams
Symphony No. 4 in F Minor by Vaughan-Williams
Symphony No. 1 by Barber
Symphony No. 5 ("Sinfonia Sacra") by Hanson
Symphony No. 6 by Schuman
Symphony No. 3 by Copland
Symphony No. 3 by Harris
Symphony No. 4 by Piston

Suggestions for Additional Comparative Studies

The *Sacred Service* by Bloch and *Threni* ("Lamentations of Jeremiah The Prophet") by Stravinsky

Works entitled *Magnificat*, by Palestrina, Buxtehude, Bach, and Vaughan-Williams

Works entitled *Stabat Mater*, by Palestrina, Vivaldi, Rossini, and Dvôrák

Don Quichotte a Dulcinee by Ravel and *Don Quixote* by Richard Strauss

German Dances by Mozart, *Invitation To The Dance* by Weber, any of the waltzes by Chopin, and *La Valse* by Ravel

Within the broad classifications of style mentioned in the preceding paragraphs, certain details of style are worthy of study on the part of the academically talented student. The harmonic idiom of the "Nocturne" from Mendelssohn's *Incidental Music to A Midsummer Night's*

51

Dream may be contrasted with that of another nocturne, *Night Soliloquy* by Kent Kennan. The rhythmic characteristics of music from Hungary, Spain, and Brazil also may be compared. In this connection, it may be helpful to study the *Suite from Háry János* by Kodály, *The Three-Cornered Hat* by de Falla and the *Bachianas Brasileiras No. 1* by Villa-Lobos.

In a comparative study of the harmonic idioms characteristic of various styles, the academically talented student may profit by writing an essay explaining the meaning of the sentence: "There is no such thing as dissonance; it is all new consonance." References to particular compositions, illustrative of specific points, will increase the educative value of preparing the essay.

PHYSICAL MEDIA
OF MUSICAL
COMMUNICATION

The medium through which music communicates—sound—has certain physical properties, mathematical relationships, and autochthonous perceptual characteristics which properly may be given some study by the academically talented student. It is understood, however, that his major experiences in music education should be related to music as an art, for an understanding of the scientific and mathematical bases of music is musically educative only to the degree to which it contributes toward the understanding and appreciation of the art of music.

Some of the relationships which exist between music and other disciples such as physics, physiology, mathematics, and psychology may be obvious. The integration of music with other subject matter areas, which is often strained, if not spurious, becomes significant only when efforts are directed toward identifying those relationships which are apparent and valid.

Among the academically talented students there will be many whose major area of interest and study lies in the sciences and mathematics. It may be assumed that for many of these students an examination of some of the psychophysical properties of musical sound would prove to be interesting and rewarding. It has been shown that some students, formerly indifferent to music, have been so intrigued by the "science" of music that study in this area has subsequently led them toward a greater appreciation of music as an art.

The concepts and skills to be developed in this area must necessarily be limited in scope and depth. For example, much of the study of acoustics has little or nothing to do with music, *per se*. Again, care must always be taken to make clear the relationship between the item under study and the perception of music. A study of acoustics can be instructive with reference to the physical nature of sound, but to expect it to give us insight into those aspects of music which are artistic would im-

ply that art can be equated with physical nature and
music with physics.

The following paragraphs contain some pertinent topics for study by the academically talented student with
a special interest in science or mathematics.

PHYSICAL AND PSYCHOLOGICAL ELEMENTS OF MUSICAL SOUND

This may include the relation of frequency and pitch,
intensity and loudness, wave form and timbre or tone
quality, and duration and time. Correlated closely with
wave form and timbre are the harmonic series, enhar-
monics, and the distinction between noise and tone.

SIMPLE ACOUSTICS

Study may be made of the generation of sound waves
by reeds, strings, edge tones, and vibrating plates and
membranes, and the action of the vocal mechanism in
singing. Such study should be accompanied by copious
illustrations of how the acoustics of instruments have
influenced and continue to influence the composer, performer, and listener.

TRANSMISSION OF SOUND

Included here may be a study of the transmission of
sound through air, the reflection and absorption of sound
waves, and the characteristics of good auditory en-
vironments.

THE AUDITORY PROCESS

This area of study may include some description of
the physical structure of the ear and the limits of auditory perception in relation to pitch and loudness. Closely

related are such autochthonous properties of musical perception as interval effects, masking, combination tones, and the nonlinear response of the ear to the perception of changes in intensity and frequency.

SCALE AND INTERVAL CONSTRUCTION

Emphasis should be placed on the cultural derivation of scales and their use. Some historical examples of scale development in the Western world may be contrasted with scales of other cultures, many of which have smaller intervals than ours. The mathematical ratios of intervals and the application of mathematical formulas in tuning and the construction of instruments may also be demonstrated.

The mathematical relationships of the vibrations of the fifth degree of a scale to those of its first degree, and the resolution of the former to the latter which is its harmonic "generator," may be an interesting and profitable subject for study, not only by students academically talented in mathematics and science, but by musically talented young people who are studying music theory. Within a given key, the natural resolution (when in a major triad) of the mediant to the submediant, the submediant to the supertonic, the supertonic to the dominant, the dominant to the tonic (III-VI-II-V-I), and the parallel relationship between keys provide an interesting manifestation of this basic mathematical relationship.

RECORDING, REPRODUCTION, AND BROADCAST OF MUSIC

Without delving deeply into electronics, an attempt may be made to help the academically talented student find information which would be useful to him as an intelligent consumer of such equipment. He may wish to know about some of the techniques of recording and reproducing music, what "high fidelity" is, the effect of nonlinear response of such apparatus and, perhaps more importantly, the effect of such mass media of communication on American musical life. It is important for the academically talented student to understand that the purpose of "high fidelity" equipment is to communicate music more clearly, and that equipment which makes it possible to hear inner parts in a piece of music is wasted unless the listener pays conscious attention to those parts.

VII

MUSIC IN
CONTEMPORARY LIFE

The academically talented student should develop an intelligent recognition of the nature and comparative values of the varied types and functions of music which are a part of virtually every phase of contemporary human activity. Mechanically reproduced music is used in trains, in airplanes, in restaurants, sometimes even in banks and in some of the better clothing shops, to induce a feeling of relaxation and well-being. Quite possibly the number of people who drive their cars to the accompaniment of music exceeds those who do not.

It is probable that music lulled the academically talented student to sleep when he was an infant, that it will add an emotional overtone to his wedding, and that it will bring comfort to those he leaves behind at the time of his funeral. In connection with his wedding, it is to be hoped that he will have acquired sufficient taste as a part of his musical education to recognize that "Dedication" by Robert Franz, Grieg's "Ich Liebe Dich," or some similar song of equal merit can bring a finer musical quality to this important occasion than "Because" or "I Love You Truly," to say nothing of "To Each His Own."

An investigation of contemporary uses of music will reveal a range from the banal musical jingles of singing commercials to the use, as a part of worship, of music which expresses the loftiest ideals of which the student is capable. Since it is to be expected that the academically talented student will take a place of leadership in the congregation of his choice, as well as in other activities of his society, it is also to be hoped that his education in music will have provided him with enough sensitivity to musical quality to enable him to use his leadership wisely, e.g., to help eliminate music that is trivial in melody and rhythm from services of worship and to substitute for it music of a quality appropriate to the high level of experience that should characterize worship.

The use of music in industry may be a suitable topic for investigation. This will include statistics on the relative output of industry when workers are listening to music and when they are not.

The increasingly knowledgeable and effective use of music for purposes of therapy in hospitals, schools, and various institutions which serve those who are physically handicapped, or emotionally and mentally disturbed, should be an intriguing and enlightening subject for investigation. This topic will be of particular value to the academically talented student whose special interest area is psychology, medicine, or psychiatry. In this connection, the academically talented student and his teacher are referred to an article entitled "Functional Music" by E. Thayer Gaston,[1] and to the 1957, 1958, and 1959 Yearbooks of the National Music Therapy Association, which are published in Lawrence, Kansas.

In the school itself, the academically talented student may participate with others in singing school songs, but he may, at the same time, be analyzing the way in which music functions to arouse school spirit. This, in turn, may lead to an investigation of the way in which music has been used to intensify patriotic fervor. In this connection, it is desirable for him to understand that music tends to emotionalize any situation of this type in which it is used. For example, there is likely to be a greater intensity of feeling involved in the singing of the national anthem or "America, the Beautiful" than there is in the recitation of the pledge of allegiance to the flag.

The young high-school graduate who, early in his Navy duty, found himself standing watch alone in absolute darkness and who, out of his memory, could hear in his head themes from great music he had learned in school, discovered that there are some things "you *can* take with

---

[1] Gaston, E. Thayer. "Functional Music." *Basic Concepts in Music Education.* Fifty-Seventh Yearbook, Part I, National Society for the Study of Education. Chicago: University of Chicago Press, 1958. Chapter 12, p. 292-309.

you." It is important for academically talented students to recognize that music can function in their lives as an inner source of beneficence if their contact with it has been constant enough and deep enough to give them a sense of self-identification with it. This can be a truly great function of music in life.

MUSICAL ACTIVITIES IN COMMUNITY LIFE

In every community there is musical activity that is significant to the people who live there. The academically talented student should investigate all the musical activities that have importance in his own community. He should understand their purposes, problems, and means of support, both financial and otherwise. As a future leader in his community, he should both investigate and think creatively about ways in which these activities could be strengthened. The musical activities in a given community may include music in a public school or college, a chamber music group, a community symphony orchestra, an opera company or other group, or a series of concerts presented by resident or itinerant artists, or both. Personal contacts with civic and musical leaders in the community, and with artists, can be both revealing and highly stimulating.

Policies of local radio and television stations with reference to the scheduling of music, commercial or serious, may be investigated and evaluated. In this connection, it can be highly instructive for the academically talented student to make a study of the scope and extent of the commercial promotion of so-called "popular" music. The reasons, musical and otherwise, why a given piece of music reaches the "top ten," and why it may, with equal suddenness, depart therefrom is another interesting area for exploration.

If the academically talented student's investigation into the presentation of concert artists in his community has included the area of practices in booking, he will have discovered that his community cannot function altogether independently in such matters and that it necessarily must present its concerts according to one or another of the few systems of booking that are national in scope. In this connection, the academically talented student is referred to *Worlds of Music* by Cecil Smith.[2]

Since, in our society, the musical activities of one community are interrelated with those of other communities, and since the academically talented student should be acquainted with the nature and scope of musical activities throughout his native land, his investigation of music in contemporary life should be national in scope. In this connection, we may cite the following facts (*circa* 1960):

1. More money is spent in our country for tickets to concerts than for tickets to baseball games.
2. There are more than 1100 instrumental groups throughout the United States that are known as "symphonic" or "philharmonic" orchestras. Of these, 22 have annual budgets in excess of $250,000 and some budgets approach $2,000,000.
3. These orchestras involve the participation of approximately 70,000 players and of 80,000 volunteer workers who serve on boards and committees.
4. Approximately 7800 concerts of symphonic music are presented each year, with an estimated annual attendance of 10,000,000 people.
5. Approximately 30 percent of the orchestras exist in communities in which the population is less than 25,000. Of all the cities in the United States with a population of 50,000 or more, less than a dozen are without a symphonic ensemble of some kind.

[2] Smith, Cecil. *Worlds of Music*. Philadelphia: J. B. Lippincott Co., 1952. p. 9-128.

6. The foregoing facts would seem to indicate that the symphonic orchestra is the keystone on which serious musical development in the United States is based.[3]
7. It has been reported that in 1958 there were 728 organizations, only half of them in educational institutions, producing opera in the United States. During the 1957-58 season, almost 4000 performances of opera were presented in the United States.[4]

Since more than half of the country's high-school children live in communities of 75,000 or more people,[5] an investigation into activities of the type mentioned above can provide significant learning for very large numbers of academically talented students, many of whom may be expected to be leaders in these communities. For further information concerning this general topic, the academically talented student and his teacher are referred to *Music in American Life* by Jacques Barzun.[6]

MUSICAL ACTIVITIES DURING THE SUMMER

Academically talented students and those who have exceptional ability in musical performance or composition should find it profitable to investigate the numerous musical activities that are carried on in various parts of the United States during the summer months. These

---

[3] Thompson, Helen M. *A Report on Conductors Study and Training Opportunities*. Charleston, West Va.: American Symphony Orchestra League, 1960.

[4] *Concert Music U.S.A.* Pamphlet. Sixth revised edition. New York: Broadcast Music, 1959.

[5] Michael, Lloyd S., and others. "Secondary School Programs." *Education for the Gifted*. Fifty-Seventh Yearbook, Part II, National Society for the Study of Education. Chicago: University of Chicago Press, 1958. Chapter 12, p. 271.

[6] Barzun, Jacques. *Music in American Life*. Gloucester, Mass.: Peter Smith, 1958. 126 p.

are to be found in major centers of musical activity and also in comparatively smaller and more isolated places. Many of them involve opportunities for exceptional experiences in music listening. Notable examples are the Lewisohn Stadium, Tanglewood, Robin Hood Dell, Ravinia Park, Red Rocks, Aspen, Central City, and Hollywood Bowl. At some of these places, and at others where somewhat similar activities occur during the summer, the musically talented student is offered an unusually high level of instruction. Any investigation of music in American contemporary life would be incomplete without a study of their organization, purposes, and activities.

MUSIC AS ENTERTAINMENT

Academically talented students who have a genuine interest in the theater may find it useful to investigate the role of music in the contemporary American theater. Such a study should include the use of "incidental music" in connection with dramatic productions, musical comedy, and light opera. It may also include an analysis of the relative importance of musical shows and straight dramatic productions, the special problems in presenting musical shows, including budgetary matters, as well as a comparative evaluation of the musical quality of such shows as *The Gypsy Baron, Carousel, The Song of Norway,* and *Kismet,* in relation to *The Red Mill, Gypsy, Guys and Dolls, The Music Man,* and *The Sound of Music.* Similar comparisons may be made with shows that will be playing in subsequent years.

The academically talented student should understand that within the genre of the musical theater there are levels of quality, as there are in more serious music of a less commercial nature, and that, in like manner, there are contrasting levels in the quality of performances by various personalities in show business that parallel levels of achievement among concert artists.

IX

MUSIC
AND THE
ARTS

The education of academically talented students should include deep, rich, and meaningful experiences in other arts, as well as in music. Although virtually every human being is responsive to music in one way or another, some academically talented students will find their most significant experiences in a fine art other than music. It is no repudiation of the special qualities of music and its unique value in human life and education to suggest that if an academically talented student has a really dynamic and compelling experience in the fine arts, one which will make his life qualitatively better than it otherwise might be, the quality of that experience is of greater importance than the particular medium through which he finds it.

Unquestionably there are certain similarities among the arts. There are also obvious differences. To over-emphasize either serves no useful purpose. Thoughtful consideration of both similarities and differences among several arts can clarify concepts, relative to each, that are important for the academically talented student to understand.

The special intellectual capacities of academically talented students make it appropriate for them to consider relationships among the arts, for they are particularly capable in conceptual learning, problem solving, and in thinking creatively about relationships among ideas. It is important, however, that studies in this field be characterized by the utmost authenticity. Too often there is a tendency to reach out to left field for a distant relationship when the closer and, therefore, better one will be found near home base.

The academically talented student should understand that the most fundamental common denominator among the arts is to be found in the basic human urges that have brought them into being and have sustained their development for as long as civilization has existed. These urges arise from man's innate craving for beauty and from those aspects of his nature which reach outward from himself in an effort to idealize many aspects of his living. Throughout history, human beings have turned to the arts for experiences with which their feelings, aspirations, ideals, and dreams could be identified. Thus, the arts are similar in the basic motivations from which they have emerged and evolved and in the most fundamental functions they perform in human life.

SIMILARITIES AMONG THE ARTS

Perhaps the most profound similarity among the arts is that each of them is expressive of values that are intrinsic. There is no material value that can be equated with the greatest works of Michelangelo, da Vinci, Rembrandt, Milton, Shakespeare, Browning, Bach, Beethoven, and Wagner. It is impossible to think of their masterpieces in materialistic terms or to find words to express their values, except to say that they are intrinsic and spiritual.

The arts are also similar in that their manifestations are ever-present in the ordinary affairs of life. We do not clothe ourselves merely for warmth; we want our clothing to have such basic elements as color, texture, line, and pattern, all of which combine to give it style. We want our food to be nutritious; but also to be flavored in an interesting manner. We expect our housing to be practical in terms of the uses to which it is put; but we want it also to be appealing in architectural design and in color. Various objects will be placed in this house because they have utilitarian value; but we hope that they will also fit artistically into a total scheme. A household need can be met by a ceramic; but we want it to be interesting in color, texture, and design. Thus it is that in many of the ordinary affairs of our living we crave not only the utilitarian, but the beautiful as well. To the extent that our environment is artistic, it transcends the mundane and symbolizes a level of feeling and thought above the commonplace.

Another basic similarity among the arts is the necessity for an inner logic. Whatever its medium of expression, the work of art must be consistent with itself. The necessity for an inner organic unity is common to the arts. Since an understanding of this unity necessarily includes the various constituent elements that are unified, an understanding of form is a necessity common to education in all of the arts.

Other similarities among the arts, while comparatively superficial, involve concepts which may be helpful for the academically talented student to understand. If his interest lies more in art than in music, it may be helpful for him to think of melody as the line of music, of harmony and instrumentation as the color of music, of rhythm as the way music moves, and of form as design.

If his interest is poetry, it may facilitate his understanding of music to realize that just as a meaningful succession of words makes a sentence, so a succession of tones makes a melody when it conveys melodic meaning.

Whether his particular interest is in poetry or in music, it may contribute to his understanding of both to consider thoughtfully the ideas of John Ciardi:

> One talks about the subject of a poem when he does not know what to do with the "poemness" of the poem. That "poemness" exists no where but in the poem's performance of itself, from itself, into itself. The poem is forever generating its own context. Like a piece of music, it exists as a self-entering, self-generating, self-complicating, self-resolving form. The essence of a poem is that one thing in it requires another. It is one thing pushing another across a silence. . . . Poetry is never about ideas; it is about the experience of an idea. And this is a very different thing. . . . The only way on earth of transmitting the experience of the idea rather than the idea is through its form.[1]

[1] Ciardi, John. "A Poem Talks to Itself." *Saturday Review* 12-13; January 24, 1959.

All students to some extent, and the academically talented to a much greater and deeper extent, should deal less with the subjective meaning of music, which is variable, than with the "musicness" of music, which is constant. It is true of music, as John Ciardi says of poetry, that one thing in it requires another. This is the source of its form.

DIFFERENCES AMONG THE ARTS

Although, at their deepest level, the fundamental purposes and values of the arts may be similar, there are marked differences in the media through which they communicate. The visual arts occupy three dimensions in space. They involve material objects. Music, however, exists only in time. It consists of nothing material which can occupy space and be seen by the eye. Its distinguishing characteristic is tone, which is perceived only by the ear or recalled in the mind.

Each art has its own integrity; each has its own constituent elements. The meaning of each is to be found in those elements and in the way they are used. The meaning of a work of art is artistic; the meaning of a poem is poetic; the meaning of music is musical. If an artist, a poet, and a musician choose the same subject for their creative efforts, there may be some similarity in the general effect of their results, but differences will be inevitable, for the language of each differs from the language of the others to such an extent that if an attempt is made to translate from one to the other, the meaning necessarily becomes different.

INTERRELATIONSHIPS AMONG THE ARTS

Certain broad stylistic tendencies among the arts are sufficiently related to justify thoughtful attention on the part of the academically talented student. A study of the expressive purposes of painters, poets, and musicians who were romanticists, and of their works, may result in an understanding of the similarities in attitude and feeling which motivated them. It may also reveal that their varied works frequently evoke a similarity of response. In addition, it can point up the contrasting media of expression, characteristic of each, in such a way that each is more clearly understood.

The academically talented student will find particularly close relationships among the arts through a study of impressionism in music and art and of symbolism in literature. A study of the music of Debussy, the paintings of Monet, Manet, and Renoir, and the writings of Mallerme and Verlaine will reveal close similarity of intent and methods that are strikingly parallel, in view of the fundamental differences in media. For example, the painters placed side by side colors which, according to the traditional rules of color, did not blend. When viewed from a distance, however, they seem to fuse together in perfect blending. Similarly, composers in the impressionistic style placed next to each other chords which, according to the traditional rules of harmony, were unrelated. These comparatively unrelated harmonic progressions of chords, in some mysterious way, give an effect of blending with the same fusion as do the colors of Monet. In like manner, the writers frequently used sequences of syllables or words which, according to traditional processes of writing, seemed to make no sense because they were unrelated in idea. Yet, a definite mood was created. In the music of Debussy, the academically talented student will find that the composer frequently used fragmentary melodies which corresponded to the short brush strokes of the painters. Effects of rhythm and orchestration were suggestive of the somewhat staccato effect of the pointillism of Seurat.

Notwithstanding all of these similarities, however, it is impossible for Debussy's *Engulfed Cathedral* to convey the content of Monet's painting of the same name. It is important for the academically talented student to recognize similarities between works by Debussy and Monet in their artistic purposes and in such technical matters as have just been mentioned. But it is equally important for him to recognize and understand the inevitable differences between the two works, in terms of their inherent nature and meaning. In this connection, it might be profitable for a group of academically talented students to carry on a debate on the topic: "*Resolved,* That a visual subject can be communicated through an aural medium." (The statement may be worded in negative form.)

Academically talented students should recognize that although a painting or a poem and a musical composition may have the same title, this fact in itself does not imply inherent similarities among the arts. These students should have knowledge of musical and literary works that have been based upon the same subject, and of paintings and musical compositions that are similarly related by topic such as "The Island of the Dead" by Böcklin and Rachmaninoff. To study these works together increases the understanding of each, but the fact that they are related to the same idea does not make their essential content and nature similar. Both Pushkin and Glinka unquestionably were motivated by purposes of nationalism, but there is no inherent similarity between Pushkin's poetry and Glinka's music beyond the general similarity between poetry and music suggested by John Ciardi on page 68.

The academically talented student who is interested in either the rise of nationalism or in literary or musical expressions of tragedy may find broad similarities of feeling in the writing of Dostoevski and the music of Mussorgsky. Both are essentially somber and deeply tragic. A study of what it is in each that gives it this quality and of how each conveys its meaning should contribute to important understandings on the part of the academically talented student. It might be interesting for a group of these students to discuss a topic such as *"Resolved,* That similarities in the emotional impact of works by Dostoevski and Mussorgsky are due more to the personal characteristics and basic purposes of the two men than to inherent similarities between literature and music." (The statement could be worded in reverse.)

ORGANIZATION OF INSTRUCTION

The academically talented student may develop understandings of similarities and differences among the arts as he studies them in classes scheduled separately in each field or he may develop them in one class organized to deal with all of the arts and the relationships among them. He may participate in seminars in the arts, either during or after the school day. He may engage in independent study and research through which he will develop significant understandings in this field.

His experiences are likely to be of the highest quality in a class or seminar where "team teaching" is possible. If a teacher who is exceptionally able in the field of music is joined by an equally capable teacher in art and another in literature, the student will have the advantage of instruction which is more likely to be authentic in each field than it would be if the teacher were expert in only one field and somewhat less knowledgeable in the others. Flexibility in the assignment of teacher time is as desirable as flexibility in the scheduling of a program for the student. If the best minds among students are to deal with concepts of similarities and differences among various arts, they should have the advantage of the highest possible quality of instruction in each of them.

X

SCHEDULING

The increasing complexity of contemporary life has placed added responsibilities and pressures upon the student, the teacher, and the school of today. Young people now need greater knowledge than ever before and they need it in depth. The scope of the curriculum has been greatly expanded, and increasing demands are being made upon all students, particularly upon those with exceptional endowment. The use of time is of great importance to these students.

FLEXIBILITY OF SCHEDULING

An examination of the considerable quantity of material that has been written during the last two years concerning the education of academically talented students reveals a definite trend in the direction of greater flexibility in scheduling. Evidently, school administrators have taken a sharp look at the practice of scheduling all subjects for an identical number of periods per week. They are now moving from a policy of determining the master schedule on the basis of administrative convenience to a policy of providing the flexibility necessary for a broader and more effective educational program. Increasing attention to the needs of academically talented students is leading also to planning for flexibility in the number of subjects which these students may take.

Freedom from rigid class attendance has been reported:

> Schools where academic programming is not unduly rigid have sometimes permitted students to work "on their own" during class time. The student is regularly enrolled in a course for which he is completely responsible. Because of his special abilities, however, he is permitted to be absent from the classroom during a specified number of periods each week in order to carry on an approved individual program for independent research. This may involve working with a more advanced group, or simply availing himself of the facilities offered by the school or by the community.

74

The independent work is undertaken, of course, under the supervision of a faculty member.

Usually the research or special project is directly related to the course from which the student is periodically absent. Some schools, however, apply more liberal criteria and allow the student to pursue work completely unrelated to that class, but in keeping with his special interests and abilities. This arrangement has been found acceptable to students, administration, and teachers, provided all understand the basic principle that merely spending a certain length of time in a particular classroom is not the real goal of enrollment in a course. If, instead, the true criterion is mastery and comprehension of the subject matter involved, everyone concerned will be able to look at the practice with an understanding and accepting attitude.[1]

Thus, there is a growing recognition of the fact that it is unrealistic to presume that all subjects should have the same time allotment per week. Some subjects can be adapted to a schedule which calls for meetings of only two or three days a week. If there are a sufficient number of these subjects, students can program two of them during one period. Such subjects might include foreign language, mathematics, physical education, typing, music, art, home economics, and industrial arts. An arrangement of this kind can give greater flexibility to the schedule and permit the academically talented student to choose electives in accordance with his talents and interests. Under the hour-long, six-period day schedule, gifted students seldom have time for free electives in the art fields, unless they use summer-school study and out-of-school seminars to free their schedules.

Another possibility for saving time for more electives is to offer some subjects, such as art, music, home economics, industrial arts, science, and other laboratory-

[1] National Education Association, National Association of Secondary-School Principals. *Administration—Procedures and School Practices for the Academically Talented Student.* Washington, D. C.: the Association, a department of the National Education Association, 1960. p. 93.

75

type classes in double periods. Because of the time spent during each class period in setting up and putting away materials and equipment, two full double periods per week are equal to approximately the same amount of instructional time as five standard single periods.

Apart from the master schedule of the school, academically talented students can be given varying degrees of latitude with respect to their own schedules. For example, on the basis of individual ability and interest, it should be possible to permit a given student to share one period between two subjects. In the traditional schedule, the academically talented student is often bored because of repetitive activities which are carried on for the benefit of the student of lesser ability. These activities seldom are of value to the academically talented student. Learning is not directly related to the amount of time which a student spends in a class. A superior performer should not be required to remain daily in an orchestra, band, or choir where considerable time is spent in rehearsing passages which he already knows. Such a student should be permitted to put this time to better use. It is quite possible, too, that the music class is not the only one in which he is bored and wastes time while waiting for other students to "catch up."

Frequently a student, in making out his program of courses, must choose between two subjects, thus depriving himself completely of one of the subjects for which he perhaps exhibits a keen interest or a real talent. Electives usually suffer when such choices must be made. A better practice is to permit the academically talented student to participate in both classes on an alternate day basis or to follow some other partial attendance plan agreed upon in advance. Such cases should be evaluated carefully, on an individual basis, by counselors and teachers. Experiences of this kind help the academically talented student to learn to use his time wisely and profitably. It is conceivable that some highly gifted students could be involved in 8 or 10 different subject fields during a given year.

Within the framework of the music class itself, there are additional possibilities for flexible arrangements. In the large ensemble class, interminable repetition of material which the academically talented student already knows well is a waste of time for him. This student, with guidance from the teacher, should be able to spend part of the time rehearsing with a few other selected students in a small ensemble, or be allowed to spend part of the period assisting less able students.

Some of the most talented performers, who are also academically talented, may plan to enter college as music majors, perhaps in preparation for music teaching. These students often have musical deficiencies because of their preoccupation with a single medium of musical performance. Instead of devoting each full period to the large group rehearsal, the time of selected students may be spent to better advantage in developing skill on a second instrument, learning to read from a different clef, engaging in functional piano practice, carrying out activities in music theory assigned by the teacher, or hearing and analyzing representative works in music literature that are beyond their ability to perform. Such individual activities constitute a legitimate use of practice rooms. Too often these facilities in modern high schools are poorly used or not used enough to justify their existence.

If band and orchestra meet during the same period, the best wind players can participate in both groups. This provides students with the opportunity to become better acquainted with twice as much musical literature as could be learned in only one group. There are also possibilities for the academically talented student to have both vocal and instrumental experiences during the same period. Instrumental students are often deprived of any opportunities to sing because of schedule problems. Flexibility in programming within the music department can frequently solve this problem for individual students, e.g., by permitting them to participate in both a choral and an instrumental class during the same period.

THE ROLE OF THE TEACHER

The trend is in the direction of a longer day, more periods per day, greater flexibility in the scheduling of those periods, and in the use of time outside of school for seminars and independent study. We should be eager to contribute to this movement in every possible way. The time is at hand for teachers of music, who are traditionally among the most devoted of professional educators, to be resourceful, imaginative, and energetic in promoting every possible scheme that will broaden and deepen the musical experiences of all students, and those of the academically talented, in particular.

This may call for some unselfishness in certain quarters. It may not be quite so pleasant to conduct a rehearsal of a large vocal or instrumental performing group without the best performers for one or two days per week, but it is quite possible that those who remain in the group will develop greater independence and confidence because they are thrown on their own resources. The best performers, in turn, may be having other types of musical experiences, which should make them more knowledgeable participants upon returning to the group.

Excellence of achievement in one particular form of musical performance is, of course, greatly to be desired and respected, but too many of our young people who perform skillfully have only the most meager concepts of the background, content, form, or expressive significance of what they are performing. Let teachers of music be certain that they are as willing to be flexible in permitting their students a diversity of musical experience within a given period as they expect their administrators to be in promoting flexibility in the master schedule.

Lloyd S. Michael, in the Fifty-Seventh Yearbook of the National Society for the Study of Education, expressed a similar point of view in the following statement:

> More flexible programming in high school can often make it possible for a student to participate in several music groups during a given semester. When he has a high degree of talent, it is not always necessary for him to engage in all the rehearsal activities of each group. Too often our most gifted musicians are held to a single musical activity all through high school. A fine instrumentalist should also be able to participate in vocal classes. A talented trumpet player might divide his time between band and chorus during a given period by singing in the choral group, serving as accompanist, or acting as assistant to the teacher. Players of wind instruments can often be programmed so that they play in both band and orchestra, spending only half-time in each group.
>
> Gifted music students are often motivated by being given opportunities to assist with teaching. They can assist the regular teacher in conducting rehearsals of large groups, directing sectional rehearsals, or directing small ensembles which may be established on an extracurriculum basis. In some localities, such students are permitted to teach, under supervision, in the summer music programs sponsored by the school system.[2]

---

[2] Michael, Lloyd S., and others, *op. cit.*, p. 307.

XI

THE MUSIC
TEACHER OF THE
ACADEMICALLY TALENTED

The Educational Policies Commission of the National Education Association has recommended that the teacher of the gifted have "superior intelligence; a rich fund of information; versatility of interests; an inquiring mind; ability to stimulate and inspire; modesty and a sense of social and professional responsibility; freedom from jealousy; freedom from excessive sensitivity to criticism; understanding of educational psychology with special knowledge of the psychology of gifted children." [1]

In the rapidly increasing body of literature concerning the education of academically talented and gifted students, there is gradually emerging a consistency of judgment that the best minds among our students deserve the best teachers, and that special qualifications and special training are necessary to teach academically talented students successfully.

A recent study by Frank T. Wilson showed that "29% and 31% of city elementary and secondary school superintendents and 26% and 30% of state elementary and secondary school superintendents were in favor of special preparation." [2] A study by Cole and Fliegler reported that 79 percent of teachers working with the gifted believed special training essential. [3] Abraham found a similar point of view among administrators. [4]

But special training is not enough. If children are to be inspired to do their best, their teacher must be inspirational. He must believe in what he teaches and communicate this belief with enthusiasm. Without being overly zealous, he must be intensely convinced that

[1] National Education Association, National Association of Secondary-School Principals, *op. cit.*, p. 125.

[2] Wilson, Frank T. "Preparation for Teachers of Gifted Children in the United States." *Exceptional Children* 20: 78-80; November 1953.

[3] Cole, Isa, and Fliegler, Louis A. *The XL Program in Action: An Evaluation.* Syracuse: Syracuse University, 1959.

[4] Abraham, Willard. "Administrators Look at Gifted Children." *Educational Administration and Supervision* 43: 280-84; May 1957.

what he is teaching is worth learning, and he must have the persuasiveness and skill to motivate his students to share this belief and act upon it.

The learning situation in the classroom takes on a particularly dynamic quality when the teacher has a sense of discovery along with his pupils. The teacher of exceptional knowledge, skill, creativity, and confidence can stimulate his pupils to great effort if he has personal characteristics which enable him to work with them as partners in an educational venture. If the academically talented student is to maintain intellectual curiosity, an inner drive to learn, and a sense of joy and satisfaction in learning, his teacher must possess and convincingly exemplify the same characteristics. In fact, the teacher of the academically talented student must himself continue to be a student if he is to be successful. One course taught by such a teacher is more valuable than a variety of courses taught by teachers less qualified.

MUSICAL QUALIFICATIONS

In teaching music to academically talented students, the qualifications cited, although they are essential, will be insufficient unless they are matched by musicianship of an exceptionally high order. The teacher of music must be a musician of such accomplishment, erudition, and taste that he can win the respect of his most capable students and also of the musical leaders in his community, upon whom he will need to call for special services to assist his students.

It is important that his skill as a musician be matched by the breadth and depth of his knowledge of the literature of music and of the literature that has been written about it. He must be exceptionally well informed about numerous sources of information pertaining to music and musicians, and he must know enough to be able to

82

help his students distinguish between fact and fiction in the vast amount of material that has been written in the field. It is important that, in addition to his musical skills in performance, he possess exceptional ability to hear detail in musical performance, whether it be live or recorded. His knowledge of the history of music should be extensive and related to his knowledge of music itself. He should also have a thorough knowledge of the theoretical aspects of music and the ability to use them with both skill and creativity.

If teachers of music are to meet the special needs of academically talented students for independent research and study, they will need to draw upon an especially broad knowledge of appropriate materials which may include recordings, books, magazines, films, film strips, and research studies available in college libraries.

If his major interests lie in those aspects of music education which are not performance oriented, the teacher must, nevertheless, have a wholesome respect for performance, when it is musical. If his principal activity in teaching is with performing groups, he must be a musician of sufficient breadth to recognize the importance and value of other activities in the music education program, and have a sufficiently broad view of the purposes of music education to understand that the program exists for the pupil, rather than the pupil existing for the program. He, therefore, will support the kind of flexibility in scheduling which will permit academically talented students to profit from a variety of musical experiences.

PREPARATION

The foregoing statements have definite implications with regard to the training of music teachers. These implications will be obvious to any music educator who is successfully engaged in teacher training. Specifically,

83

it is recommended that teacher-training institutions give serious consideration to the following:

1. Strict adherence to standards of musical competencies, evidenced through examinations, as a qualification for the teaching credential (rather than merely the accumulation of units)

2. Greatly increased attention to the preparation of teachers in the field of general music for all students, with special attention to this type of experience at a very high level for the academically talented student

3. A re-examination of the curriculum to ensure that there is a balance between musical performance and other courses in music education that is realistic in terms of the future work of graduates in the public schools

4. The inclusion in the music curriculum of one or more courses similar in content to those which are recommended for the academically talented student

5. The development of certain interdepartmental projects, involving psychology, education, art, and literature, which will provide, either in a specialized course or within existing courses, the knowledge from each of those fields that is necessary for successful work with academically talented students.

It is to be hoped that leaders in music education, in teacher-training institutions, will encourage those of their students who are themselves academically talented to prepare to work with academically talented students. Today, there is a great need for specialization in music education outside the field of performance. It is imperative that this need be met if music is to maintain its rightful place in the curriculum in public education.

SPECIAL NEEDS

In addition to the usual supplies and equipment provided for the regular activities of a music department, the teacher who is working with academically talented students has special needs, which include the following:

1. An ample number of phonographs, or turntables with earphones, to provide for independent listening
2. An especially large library of recordings, conductor's scores, books, magazines, and films—and time to study them in depth
3. Time for research and preparation, at his own level, to ensure his own continuing growth as a musician and teacher
4. Time for personal interviews with academically talented students who are engaged in individual projects
5. Time and opportunity to visit other schools which are involved in similar projects, and for attendance at meetings and conventions where problems pertaining to the musical and general education of the academically talented student are discussed
6. A feeling that his administrators and supervisors recognize his problems, support his efforts, appreciate his successes, and provide every possible assistance to him in working with academically talented students.

XII

MUSIC EDUCATION FOR THE MUSICALLY TALENTED OR GIFTED

The musically *gifted* student ranks among the top 2 to 3 percent of all students throughout the country in musical ability. He may be intellectually gifted as well, and is likely to be academically talented. He is not to be found in every school at a given time. There are times when he is not to be found in any school at all, and it is unlikely, though not impossible, that several of these incredibly exceptional young people will be found in any school at the same time. This student is the concert artist of tomorrow. He is the important composer or conductor of the future. His musical gifts arouse a sense of mystery and wonder. Even the most exceptionally superior teacher is confronted with awesome responsibilities in having such a young person as a student. It is impossible to do enough for this pupil. It is for him, above all other students, that every possible concession should be made in scheduling, in order to provide him with both a broad basic education and time for the concentration of effort which is necessary if he is to achieve his potential greatness.

The musically *talented* student is among the upper 20 to 25 percent of all students in terms of musical capacity and ability. His gifts are not as exceptional as those of the gifted student, but they are of a high level. He, too, is likely to be academically talented. He has the capacity for a successful career in some form of musical activity, but is not at all certain to pursue it. If he is academically talented, he probably possesses the potentiality for a successful career in music teaching, and if he has appropriate personal qualities, he should be encouraged in that direction. This student is likely to bring joy to his teacher, and he, too, presents a challenge to his school in terms of providing him with a breadth and depth of musical experience commensurate with his talents.

IDENTIFICATION OF THE MUSICALLY GIFTED OR TALENTED

Identification of the musically gifted student in the senior high school is virtually unavoidable, for the manifestations of his extraordinary gifts will already have become unmistakable. It is possible, however, that among the musically talented there are those, truly gifted in composing, whose gifts are not yet evident. It is important that musically talented young people be encouraged and given every opportunity to engage in creative work so that exceptional creative gifts may be discovered.

It is more difficult to identify, with reliability, the musical talents of a young person than it is to identify his intellectual potentiality. Numerous reports, representing various parts of the country, indicate that although certain formal tests are available and in use here and there, the most widely accepted evidences of musical talent are interest and achievement. In this connection, De Haan and Wilson have made the following statement:

> It is important to discover a wide variety of abilities besides intellectual ability. Some of these other abilities are artistic aptitudes of all kinds. . . . These aptitudes are not always clearly defined and are often made up of a combination of abilities, interests and social and personal factors. . . . In the fine arts it is not yet possible to separate achievement from aptitude, and tests in these areas measure both to some extent at the same time.[1]

In his chapter on "The Characteristics and Objectives of a Program for the Gifted," Clifford W. Williams writes:

> Methods of identifying children with particular talents are still considerably less objective than the methods of selecting the intellectually gifted. Talent testing in the

---

[1] De Haan, Robert F., and Wilson, Robert C. "Identification of the Gifted." *Education for the Gifted.* Fifty-Seventh Yearbook, Part II, National Society for the Study of Education. Chicago: University of Chicago Press, 1958. Chapter 9, p. 169-170.

areas of art, music, and mechanics is so closely tied to experience that it is difficult to detect ability in children who have received little or no training. Qualities such as persistence and originality may give as strong indications of unusual aptitude as quality of performance.[2]

GUIDANCE AND COUNSELING

Regardless of whether the musically talented student is identified by formal tests or by informal evaluation of his achievement by his teachers, it is important that there be effective interaction between the music teacher and the counselor. In this connection, Dr. Joseph Saetveit, Supervisor of Music for the State of New York, has contributed the following statement:

> The pupil's cumulative record should include all possible indications of interests and activities in music and the other arts. Out-of-school activities, such as private lessons in piano, participation in a church choir or being selected to perform in a regional or all-state music festival should be included in the record as well as all school activities. Results of special tests, auditions or competitions should be noted.
>
> The responsibility for guidance in the arts should be shared by the guidance counselor and the teachers of music and art. When pupils of exceptional ability are discovered, the teacher of the subject area involved has a special responsibility for giving the pupil a comprehensive picture of the vocational and avocational opportunities available. Pertinent facts and figures for each vocation should be presented without bias or dictation. Further insight into various aspects of careers can be gained by reading college catalogs, by studying vocational and scholarship information in the guidance office, by conferring with college representatives, and by visiting colleges, universities and schools of art and music.
>
> The teacher should also discuss with each pupil who shows exceptional promise the courses, organizations and

---

[2] Williams, Clifford W. "Characteristics and Objectives of a Program for the Gifted." *Education for the Gifted.* Fifty-Seventh Yearbook, Part II, National Society for the Study of Education. Chicago: University of Chicago Press, 1958. Chapter 8, p. 155.

activities in the school curriculum that will help him. Pupils possessing unusual musical talent should be encouraged to participate in one or more major musical organizations, to compose or arrange music, to perform frequently in classes, school assemblies and festivals, to serve as chairman for sectional rehearsals and to assist in the planning, staging and directing of concerts and other musical productions. Those who appear to have an aptitude for teaching should be given an opportunity to observe or even to serve as assistant teachers and assistant conductors in their own classes.

Many of the above objectives can best be achieved by means of individual pupil conferences or interviews. Reports of such meetings and the recommendations made should be discussed with the guidance couselor and filed with the cumulative records of the pupils in the guidance office. Further reports of the effectiveness of the recommendations and of significant anecdotes should also be turned over to the counselor. In some schools it may be advantageous to have a duplicate file in the music department.

Throughout the process of guiding all pupils, music teachers and guidance counselors should work together. The teachers should make use of all the information and expert advice of trained counselors and should at the same time place at the disposal of their counselors their knowledge of individual pupils and of new developments in music and other arts.

THE INSTRUCTIONAL PROGRAM

In an earlier section of this publication, it is recommended that the academically talented student who is also talented in musical performance continue his participation in performing groups with strictest adherence to the highest standards of repertoire, technical skill, and musicianship. The section stresses the point, however, that training in the skills of music performance must be matched by education dealing with the nature and meaning of what is performed. Since large numbers of academically talented students will not be performers,

90

this publication has emphasized learnings other than those which develop through performance alone. For those who are musically gifted or talented, the basic point of view of this publication remains applicable. Certain modifications, however, may be desirable.

It is probable that the student who is extraordinarily gifted in musical performance is already studying with a competent private teacher. If not, it is important, within the limits of professional propriety and ethics, for the teacher to work with the parents of such a student, and with the finest professional musicians available, to arrange private instruction of the utmost competence and inspiration. In some cases where students possess this level of potentiality, there should be no reluctance in approaching the finest artists in the world. It should be remembered that even such artists as Heifetz, Piatigorsky, and Rudolf Serkin accept pupils. They may be few in number, but this discussion refers to only a few.

Similar contacts are important for the student who is musically gifted in composing. Perhaps the best contacts to be made for him will be in a college or university, or he may begin studying with a skillful professional arranger and progress to studying with an outstanding teacher of composition in a university or elsewhere. In any case, no level of achievement in professional skill or in teaching is so high that the truly gifted cannot profit from association with it.

The department should provide the richest possible program of instruction in theory and harmony for the student who is especially gifted in creative work. Independent study in counterpoint and orchestration should be motivated. The department must also encourage the student's creative work by scheduling performances of his compositions and giving him opportunities to arrange choral and orchestral music for performing groups in the school. Musical organizations in the community should also be made aware of his creative work and, when it is worthy, perform it.

In relation to musical activities in the high school, the musically gifted may be encouraged to participate in performances to the extent that they contribute to *his* growth—to the extent that they are to *his* benefit. If his exceptional gifts are in an area of performance, everything possible should be done to supplement his exceptional skill with studies in the theory, literature, and history of music, in order to broaden his musical understanding.

A program of music education for the musically talented should be well balanced between performance, the study of theory and harmony, and the study of literature and history of music. If the musically talented student is also academically talented, there are numerous areas of study that may be appropriate for him, many suggested throughout this publication. If he is not academically talented, it may be possible to select, from the suggested content, those types of learning most suited to his intellectual capacity and to relate them, as closely as possible, to the particular type of musical performance which will probably be the dominant feature of his study. This student should be encouraged to identify himself with musical activities and personalities in his community, including those in available universities and colleges.

XIII

STRENGTHENING THE
EXISTING PROGRAM

Any plan to strengthen the existing program of musical education must begin with an evaluation of the program in terms of the needs of the students who are, or should be, participating in it. This evaluation necessarily must be made at the local level by the administrators, supervisors, and teachers who are responsible for the program.

The music educator should be certain that his program is consistent with the best philosophy he knows and with the highest standard value and quality in both music and education. Upon this foundation he can enlist increased support, financial and otherwise, from his administration and his community, for he will be able to approach them with known values which will add strength to the program and are, in fact, deserving of support.

The existing program will be strengthened as the music educator eliminates from it those activities which leave it vulnerable to the charge of being a frill.

The existing program of music education will also be strengthened to the extent that it emphasizes activities and standards consistent with the current emphasis upon quality, minimizes activities that are nothing more than entertainment, and offers a program of real substance which can maintain a place of integrity with academic subjects in the total curriculum. A program of such quality provides a valid basis upon which to encourage the administration to provide sufficient flexibility of programing to enable more students to participate in it.

Perhaps no single development could add greater strength to the existing program than improvement and emphasis upon a program of general music for all pupils. In this connection, it is important for the music educator to think his way through to a real understanding of the values of general music, to seek out new materials, and to devise new methods which will make general music a dynamic, compelling experience that is musi-

94

cally justifiable and educationally valid for all students. Such a program for all students will have less depth than the program recommended for academically talented students, but it may have equal breadth. Its emphasis should be upon the general student as a consumer of music. It may place less emphasis upon education geared toward responsibilities of musical leadership, but it will be a program in which substantial learning takes place in a musically dynamic classroom situation.

The existing program of music education would also be greatly strengthened by a sharp increase in the number of teachers who specialize in general music.

In considering the existing program and suggestions for strengthening it, Dr. Paul Van Bodegraven has offered the following statement:

The Existing Program

Choral and instrumental organizations constituting the entire program of music in the majority of high schools today, have attracted a large number of academically talented students with a high degree of aesthetic interest. Many also have shown marked artistic ability. In the rigorous intellectual climate being planned for these students, it would seem more vital than ever that avenues for satisfying experiences in the search for beauty be kept open and that experiences in the art areas be made as rewarding as possible. It is likely that in the future, as in the past, performing groups will bear the largest share of responsibility for providing such experiences in music. Those groups which have been stimulating and satisfying for the academically talented student, and others, have incorporated many of the following practices into their rehearsal periods:

1. They have aimed for the highest level of musical performance of which the group and its teacher are capable. The end has been not only fine performance but, also, the development of judgment concerning essentials of good performance of which each group member must become aware as he helps to raise the level, day by day, and month by month. A fine performance is transitory; the ability to make good judgments is lasting.

2. They have a carefully selected repertoire of a wide variety of the best musical literature available. There is an awareness of the primary importance of exposure to and study of material with intrinsic musical value as the basis for the growth of a discriminating judgment in the selection of musical experiences through a lifetime.

3. They have used this wide variety of musical literature as a basis for:

 a. Developing an understanding of theory and increasing skill in its use in music reading.

 b. Creating an awareness of the historical periods in music and the stylistic practices which distinguish each period, particularly in varying uses of melody, harmony, rhythm, form, instrumentation and tone color.

 c. Developing the ability to understand and use musical terms. Such terms, rather than their "translations", are used freely when giving directions during rehearsals.

4. They have provided special opportunities for gifted students to appear as soloists, student conductors, section leaders, assistant teachers, and as members of small ensembles.

Strengthening the Present Program

Certain possibilities exist for strengthening performing organizations so that they may better serve the academically talented and others. Only those which are concerned with administration are mentioned here:

1. Support and encourage performing groups in their efforts to incorporate into their programs, the aforementioned practices.

2. Continue a study of improved scheduling practices which will make it possible for any student to elect work in music during his entire school lifetime. This may involve adopting an eight period day or other arrangements of scheduling.

3. Formulate a policy governing performances outside of regular school activities which will permit the groups to be operated primarily as an educational experience for the participants.

4. Encourage the full development (or establishment) of the mixed chorus and orchestra, two groups for which some of the world's greatest music has been written.

5. Support and encourage the formation of smaller performing groups in addition to or instead of one large group where such action would result in groups more evenly matched in ability and achievement.

XIV

GUIDING
PRINCIPLES

- In music education, no other activity can substitute for direct experience with music, through performing or listening. Contact with music is the one indispensable foundation for musical growth.

- Reading about music, analyzing it, and discussing it have meaning only as they are related to music which already has been heard or to tonal concepts that are clearly in the mind as a result of silent reading of musical notation.

- The varying musical interests which individual academically talented students may wish to pursue require provision for a variety of activities. Mere variety, however, will not meet their needs. A program of music education for these exceptional students is validated less by the number and diversity of its activities than by the quality and depth of learning that results from them.

- Although the music education of academically talented students should be intellectually oriented, it should also help them to develop emotionally. These students deserve experiences that will evoke ever-deepening responses from both the mind and the heart.

- Content and instruction in music education must never confirm the notion that music activities are "easy." Such a notion tends to discourage the brightest students from the study of music. Music education must be both intellectually challenging and emotionally compelling.

- There is no place in music education for any rehearsal or classroom experience which is merely routine. This should be avoided in any situation—with academically talented students it is deplorable. Similarly, there is no justification in music education for any type of busy work. Collections of pictures and articles have little, if any, value. To the extent, however, that a series of articles about a given topic is organized so as to indicate the development of a significant concept concerning music, it is of educational value.

- The social attitudes, habits, and status to be derived from musical activities may have validity as an outcome of music education, but they are not its purpose. Were they to be regarded as the purpose, the content could easily be so lacking in organization and continuity that little, if any, musical growth would result.

- The ability to hear everything there is to be heard in a piece of music and to understand how each part of it is related to the other parts is of greater value than memorized knowledge of biographical data concerning its composer.

- The academically talented student should be given every encouragement and opportunity to participate in creative activities and in independent study.

PERFORMING GROUPS

The academically talented student whose musical experience qualifies him to participate in selective performing groups should participate in them, provided they include opportunity for learnings other than performance skills. These other learnings should include an understanding of form, harmonic idiom, the expressive significance of the music he is rehearsing, and other factors that may have helped to determine the nature of the music. If the rehearsals of the performing group do not provide for learnings other than performing skills, the academically talented student should enroll in courses, independent study groups, honors classes, or seminars which meet during or after the school day. These activities are essential for his growth in understanding the nature and meaning of music.

100

Students who play an instrument or sing should be provided with the opportunity to hear parts other than their own and to understand the interrelationships between these parts. When a passage is repeated in rehearsal, it should be for a definite purpose which is understood by the students, so that with each repetition the passage is improved. The academically talented student will require much less repetitive drill than other students. When he is able to perform the music correctly, he should be free to participate in some other form of musical activity more instructive to him. Not to permit this is to waste the time of academically talented students, which is one of the most valuable assets of this nation.

Academically talented students, allowed to serve as assistant conductors or assistant teachers, strengthen their own learning as they attempt to teach others, develop social competence in leadership and a taste for teaching which may encourage them toward a career in this field.

These students cannot be expected to remain in performing organizations semester after semester if their experiences continue to be simply "more of the same." In addition to a different repertoire, they have a right to expect that something new will be added in terms of more advanced ear-training, increasing understanding of theory, and associative concepts which will both broaden and deepen their musical understandings. The fact that this may be difficult to achieve, with new students enrolling each semester, simply serves to emphasize the necessity for flexibility in scheduling. Such a schedule will make it more possible, in a performing ensemble, to meet the varying needs of students with divergent abilities.

It is important for the academically talented student (as well as other students) to develop and maintain a sense of responsibility to the performing groups of which he is a part. However, it is also important to remember that the performing group is a part of the music curriculum of the school and exists to serve the needs of students, rather than to provide a vehicle through which the student will serve his school and his community. The values of public performances are fully recognized, and to the extent that they provide a goal which motivates rehearsing that is more careful than it otherwise would be, they are of value. However, to the extent that public performances consist of repertoire chosen in terms of what the prospective audience will enjoy, regardless of its intrinsic merits or its appropriateness to the musical and technical needs of the participating students, they are miseducative ventures that deprive students of high quality musical experiences.

It is important to distinguish between repertoire which is musically valid for educational purposes and repertoire which is merely entertaining. The primary purpose of music education is to be musically educative. If the resulting repertoire happens to be entertaining, well and good. If not, the public must take it as it is. The outcome of such an attitude on the part of the school may well be that the music program is likely to be on more secure ground and less likely to be regarded as a frill. Academically talented students deserve the best repertoire they are capable of performing, chosen in terms of their particular needs for musical growth and rehearsed with the utmost care.

If the performing group expects to maintain the continuing participation of the academically talented student in the 1960's, it must represent a constant quest for musical quality that challenges the best and most serious effort of which that student is capable.

LISTENING

Listening is an indispensable part of every musical activity. Members of performing groups must listen to each other in order to achieve blend of tone, accuracy of intonation, and unity of ensemble. Even the personal, emotional, and social values of participation in group performance depend upon the participant's aural recognition of the musical results he has achieved. His realization of success can come only when he has heard what he has done.

Listening is also essential in the theoretical phases of music education. Without relevance to music that has been heard, a study of theory is mechanical routine, without meaning.

Listening to music should be a major part of the study of music history. The reading of factual information about music, particularly about design, and form and characteristics of style, has little, if any, significance unless it is related to direct experience with the music to which it refers.

Listening provides the individual with the opportunity to come into contact with music beyond that which he is able to perform. No matter how skilled a student or even a professional performer may be in some type of performance, his musical experiences would be tragically restricted if they were limited to those of his own performance. Virtually the entire world of music is available to the academically talented student through listening, for there is little music of importance and worth that has not been recorded. Selection of recordings for listening should be made in terms of the intrinsic worth of the music, its educative potentialities as related to the immediate needs of the student, and the quality of the performance and the recording itself.

Listening to music is not a passive experience of absorbing tone. It involves an active and responsive consciousness, one which participates with the composer and performer in an inner re-creation of a musical experience. Listening activities should be directed in such a way that they provide ample opportunities for students' responses. Properly motivated and directed listening can be an experience of discovery. Students, particularly the academically talented, should be given the fullest possible opportunity to participate in discussion, which can be followed by analysis, reading, and repeated contact with the music.

MUSIC HISTORY

The facts of music history should be related to direct experience with the music to which they refer.

For the academically talented student, comprehension in depth of a variety of music, representative of various styles, may be more important than a comparatively superficial survey of the chronology of music history.

Likewise, an understanding of the way in which the music of one composer evolved from that of his predecessors and, in turn, led to that of his successors, is more important than such biographical data as the exact dates of his birth and death or the number and details of his amours.

A study of musical idioms characteristic of early periods may be motivated by approaching them through more recent works in which they are evident. For example, Gregorian chant may be approached through the *Hymn of Jesus* by Gustav Holst or Paul Creston's *Third Symphony*. The old modes may be approached through Respighi's *Concerto Gregoriano*, much of the music of the Greek Orthodox Church, and the music which Howard Hanson composed for the "Puritan" and "Maypole" scenes in his opera, *Merry Mount*. For some students, the chronology of music history will have more meaning if it is studied after experience with music which may have been approached in substantially the reverse of chronological order.

MUSIC THEORY

Theoretical concepts will have musical meaning only as they are developed in a musical context.

The sequence of activities in theoretical study is listening, singing, playing, and writing. In this way, what is written becomes directly related to its musical antecedent. The understanding of a harmonic style or idiom is best motivated and understood in relation to a composition which illustrates it, rather than through analysis of a contrived example which is isolated from a musical context.

The more closely theoretical study can be related to music literature and, through it, to the historic development of music, the more broadly educative it will be.

If the academically talented student is studying music theory, he should be encouraged to create original music, even though his harmonic "repertoire" may be limited. His capacity for creative activity may bring surprising results!

The desire to experiment with various instruments and/or to explore creatively the use of certain idioms of melody or harmony should be encouraged, but it should not substitute for learning in depth in other phases of music, except, perhaps, for those who are especially gifted creatively in music.

MUSICAL NOTATION

The process by which facility in reading notation is developed is the same for every student, no matter how gifted he is or what his grade level may be. It begins with aural experiences which convey musical meanings, and proceeds to visual perception of notation which symbolizes that meaning. The academically talented student, however, may be expected to be eager and able to deal with written symbols of notation more quickly, and to master their use more rapidly and with greater accuracy than other students. This is particularly true if he understands that these symbols serve a useful purpose in his musical experiences.

MUSIC IN RELATION TO OTHER FIELDS

Music can be of value to the academically talented student in his study of other subjects, for it can provide a "feeling tone" that sensitizes him to nuances of learning in other fields.

Academically talented students, characteristically superior in their capacity to relate ideas, can find, through music, a source of added meaning in their study of foreign languages and cultures, literature, and social studies. Music will make its best contribution to learning in these fields when its own integrity as an art is maintained.

The authenticity of a composition's relationship to other subject fields stems not from its title but from the characteristics of its constituent musical elements. To the extent that relationships between subject fields are authentic, they should be promoted. Those relationships which are spurious should not be introduced merely for the sake of correlating subject material.

The resourceful teacher of the academically talented student will not only relate music to other subject fields but will relate learnings from other areas of study to music.

CODA

It is a basic obligation of the public schools to develop the intellectual abilities of all students. This should be a particularly dominant factor in the education of the academically talented student. Accordingly, the principles, programs, and activities recommended in this publication are intellectually oriented.

There is meaning in music to be understood. It is hoped that the education of the academically talented student will help him to understand it. There are other meanings in music that are not to be understood but experienced. These meanings lie in the mysterious realms of the spirit, realms which may be approached through understanding but are entered only by spiritual intuition that transcends the rational intellect.

The basic function of music is the communication of feeling. The academically talented student, like any other human being, is a creature of feeling. We can have confidence in the irresistible power of music to reach him at the level of feeling, and in the nature of the human organism to respond at this level. This response can motivate intellectual study which, in turn, can enrich emotional response.

Great music involves content to be understood by the mind. This content conveys feeling that evokes responses from the heart. Let the thoughts of the mind and the responses of the heart be acceptable.

APPENDIX A
Conference Participants
Conference on Music for the Academically Talented
September 24-26, 1959

Conference Chairman

WILEY L. HOUSEWRIGHT   Professor of Music Education
The Florida State University
Tallahassee, Florida

Conference Participants

HELEN C. BAILEY   Associate Superintendent
The Board of Public Education
Philadelphia, Pennsylvania

FLORENCE BOOKER   Chairman, Music Department
Arlington County Public Schools
Arlington, Virginia

KARL D. ERNST   Chairman, Division of Creative Arts
Alameda State College
Hayward, California

BEATRICE B. GILKES   Chairman, Music Department
McKinley High School
Washington, D. C.

MARCUS E. HAHN   Assistant Professor, Department of
Music Education
University of Kansas
Lawrence, Kansas

WILLIAM C. HARTSHORN   Supervisor in Charge
Music Education
Los Angeles City Board of Education
Los Angeles, California

WILEY L. HOUSEWRIGHT   Professor of Music Education
The Florida State University
Tallahassee, Florida

SADIE RAFFERTY   Chairman, Department of Music
Evanston Township High School
Evanston, Illinois

WILLIAM D. REVELLI   Conductor, University of Michigan
Bands
University of Michigan
Ann Arbor, Michigan

108

DAVID R. ROBERTSON	Director, The Conservatory of Music Oberlin College Oberlin, Ohio
JOSEPH G. SAETVEIT	Supervisor of Music Education The State Education Department Albany, New York
ELEANOR TIPTON	Supervisor of Music Philadelphia Public Schools Philadelphia, Pennsylvania
PAUL VAN BODEGRAVEN	Chairman, Department of Music New York University New York, New York
CLIFFORD W. WILLIAMS	Supervisor, Gifted Child Program Portland Public Schools Portland, Oregon

APPENDIX B

Selected Bibliography

Church Music

APEL, WILLI. *Gregorian Chant.* Bloomington: Indiana University Press, 1958.

BINDER, ABRAHAM W. *Biblical Chant.* New York: Philosophical Library, 1959.

DAVISON, ARCHIBALD T. *Church Music; Illusion and Reality.* Cambridge, Mass.: Harvard University Press, 1952.

DAVISON, A. T. *Protestant Music in America.* Boston: E. C. Schirmer, 1933.

ELLINWOOD, LEONARD. *The History of American Church Music.* New York: Morehouse-Gorham, 1953.

HUME, PAUL. *Catholic Church Music.* New York: Dodd, Mead & Co., 1956.

LOVELACE, AUSTIN C., and RICE, WILLIAM C. *Music and Worship in the Church.* New York: Abingdon Press, 1960.

WERNER, ERIC. *The Sacred Bridge; The Interdependence of Liturgy and Music in Synagogue and Church During the First Millennium.* London: Dennis Dobson, Ltd., 1959.

Composers and Performers

ABRAHAM, GERALD. *On Russian Music.* New York: Charles Scribner's Sons, 1939.

ABRAHAM, GERALD, and HEAL, ERNEST. *A Hundred Years of Music.* Second edition. London: Gerald Duckworth & Co., Ltd., 1949.

ALLEN, WARREN D. *Our Marching Civilization; An Introduction to the Study of Music and Society.* Stanford, Calif.: Stanford University Press, 1943.

APEL, WILLI. *Harvard Dictonary of Music.* Cambridge, Mass.: Harvard University Press, 1944.

ASAF'EV, BORIS V. *Russian Music from the Beginning of the Nineteenth Century.* Translated by Alfred J. Swan. Ann Arbor: Published for the American Council of Learned Societies by J. W. Edwards, 1953.

BAGAR, ROBERT C., and BIANCOLLI, LOUIS. *The Complete Guide to Orchestral Music.* New York: Grosset & Dunlap, 1947.

BAGAR, ROBERT C., and BIANCOLLI, LOUIS. *The Victor Book of Operas.* New York: Simon & Schuster, 1953.

110

BARLOW, WAYNE. *Foundations of Music.* New York: Appleton-Century-Crofts, 1953.

BARZUN, JACQUES. *Music in American Life.* Garden City, L. I.: Doubleday & Co., 1956.

BARZUN, JACQUES. *Pleasures of Music.* New York: Viking Press, 1951.

BARZUN, JACQUES. *Romanticism and the Modern Ego.* Boston: Little, Brown & Co., 1943.

BEECHAM, SIR THOMAS. *A Mingled Chime; An Autobiography.* New York: G. P. Putnam's Sons, 1943.

BEKKER, PAUL. *The Story of Music.* Translated by M. D. Herter Norton and Alice Kortschah. New York: W. W. Norton & Co., 1927.

BERNSTEIN, LEONARD. *The Joy of Music.* New York: Simon & Schuster, 1959.

BIANCOLLI, LOUIS L. *The Analytical Concert Guide.* (Edited by Louis Biancolli and William S. Mann.) London: Cassell & Co., Ltd., 1957.

BIANCOLLI, LOUIS L., and PEYSER, HERBERT F. Contributions by Robert Bagar and Pitts Sanborn. Introduction by Dimitri Mitropoulos. *Masters of the Orchestra from Bach to Prokofiev.* New York: G. P. Putnam's Sons, 1954.

BOYDEN, DAVID D. *An Introduction to Music.* New York: Alfred A. Knopf, 1956.

BRIGGS, JOHN. *The Collector's Tchaikovsky and the Five.* Philadelphia: J. B. Lippincott Co., 1959.

BROCKWAY, WALLACE, AND WEINSTOCK, HERBERT. *Men of Music; Their Lives, Times, and Achievements.* Revised edition. New York: Simon & Schuster, 1958.

BROWN, CALVIN S. *Music and Literature; A Comparison of the Arts.* Athens: University of Georgia Press, 1948.

BUKOFZER, MANFRED F. *Music in the Baroque Era.* New York: W. W. Norton & Co., 1947.

CALVOCORESSI, M. D., and ABRAHAM, GERALD. *Masters of Russian Music.* London: Gerald Duckworth & Co., Ltd., 1936.

CASELLA, A. *Music in My Time.* Norman: Oklahoma University Press, 1955.

CHASE, GILBERT. *America's Music from the Pilgrims to the Present.* New York: McGraw-Hill Book Co., 1955.

CHASE, GILBERT. *A Guide to Latin-American Music.* Washington: The Library of Congress, Music Division, 1945.

CHASE, GILBERT. *The Music of Spain.* Revised second edition. New York: Dover Publications, 1959.

CHOTZINOFF, SAMUEL. *A Lost Paradise; Early Reminiscences.* New York: Alfred A. Knopf, 1955.

COOPER, GROSVENOR, editor. *Learning to Listen.* Chicago: University of Chicago Press, 1957.

COOPER, MARTIN. *French Music from the Death of Berlioz to the Death of Fauré.* New York: Oxford University Press, 1951.

COPLAND, AARON. *Music and Imagination.* Cambridge, Mass.: Harvard University Press, 1952.

COPLAND, AARON. *Our New Music.* New York: McGraw-Hill Book Co., 1941.

COPLAND, AARON. *What to Listen for in Music.* Revised edition. New York: McGraw-Hill Book Co., 1957.

CROSS, MILTON. *Complete Stories of the Great Operas.* New York: Doubleday & Co., 1948.

CULVER, CHARLES A. *Musical Acoustics.* Fourth edition. New York: McGraw-Hill Book Co., 1956.

DALLIN, LEON. *Techniques of 20th Century Composition.* Dubuque, Iowa: Wm. C. Brown Co., 1957.

DART, THURSTON. *The Interpretation of Music.* London: Hutchinson & Co., Ltd., 1954.

DAVISON, ARCHIBALD T. *Bach and Handel; The Consummation of of the Baroque in Music.* Cambridge, Mass.: Harvard University Press, 1951.

DOWNES, EDWARD. *Adventures in Symphonic Music.* New York: Farrar and Rinehart, 1944.

DOWNES, OLIN. *Olin Downes on Music; A Selection from His Writings.* (Edited by Irene Downes.) New York: Simon & Schuster, 1957.

DOWNES, OLIN. *Symphonic Broadcasts.* New York: Dial Press, 1932.

DURIYANGA, PHRA CHEN. *Thai Music.* Fourth edition. Bangkok: National Culture Institute, 1956.

EINSTEIN, ALFRED. *Essays on Music.* New York: W. W. Norton & Co., 1956.

EINSTEIN, ALFRED. *Greatness in Music.* Translated by Cesar Saerchinger. New York: Oxford University Press, 1941.

EINSTEIN, ALFRED. *Music in the Romantic Era.* New York: W. W. Norton & Co., 1947.

ERICKSON, ROBERT. Introduction by Virgil Thomson. *The Structure of Music; A Listener's Guide.* New York: Noonday Press, 1955.

EWEN, DAVID. *American Composers Today.* New York: H. W. Wilson Co., 1949.

EWEN, DAVID. *Encyclopedia of Concert Music.* New York: Hill and Wang, 1959.

EWEN, DAVID. *European Composers Today.* New York: H. W. Wilson Co., 1954.

EWEN, DAVID, editor. *From Bach to Stravinsky.* New York: W. W. Norton & Co., 1933.

EWEN, DAVID, editor. *The Book of Modern Composers*. Second edition. New York: Alfred A. Knopf, 1950.

EWEN, DAVID. *The Complete Book of 20th Century Music*. Revised edition. Englewood Cliffs, N. J.: Prentice-Hall, 1959.

EWEN, DAVID. *The Man with the Baton*. New York: Thomas Y. Crowell Co., 1936.

EWEN, DAVID. *The World of Jerome Kern; A Biography*. New York: Henry Holt & Co., 1960.

FERGUSON, DONALD N. *A History of Musical Thought*. Third edition. New York: Appleton-Century-Crofts, 1959.

FERGUSON, DONALD N. *Masterworks of the Orchestral Repertoire*. Minneapolis: University of Minnesota Press, 1954.

FERGUSON, DONALD N. *On the Elements of Expression in Music*. Minneapolis: University of Minnesota Press, 1944.

FINCK, HENRY T. *Richard Strauss; The Man and His Works*. Boston: Little, Brown & Co., 1917.

FRENCH, RICHARD F., editor. *Music and Criticism; A Symposium*. Cambridge, Mass.: Harvard University Press, 1948.

GATTI, CARLO. *Verdi, The Man and His Music*. Translated by Elisabeth Abbott. New York: G. P. Putnam's Sons, 1955.

GEE, JOHN, and SELBY, ELLIOTT. *The Triumph of Tchaikovsky*. London: Robert Hale, Ltd., 1959.

GEIRINGER, KARL. *The Music of the Bach Family*. Cambridge, Mass.: Harvard University Press, 1951.

GRAF, MAX. *Composer and Critic*. New York: W. W. Norton & Co., 1946.

GRAY, CECIL. *The History of Music*. New York: Alfred A. Knopf, 1928.

GROUT, D. J. *A Short History of Opera*. New York: Columbia University Press, 1947.

HAGGIN, BERNARD H. *Conversations with Toscanini*. Garden City, L. I.: Doubleday & Co., 1959.

HAGGIN, BERNARD H. *The Listener's Musical Companion*. New Brunswick, N. J.: Rutgers University Press, 1956.

HANSLICK, EDWARD. *The Beautiful in Music*. Translated by Gustav Cohen. (Edited by Morris Weitz.) New York: Liberal Arts Press, 1957.

HAUSER, ARNOLD. *The Social History of Art*. New York: Alfred A. Knopf, 1951.

HELL, HENRI. *Francis Poulenc*. Translated by Edward Lockspeiser. London: John Calder, Ltd., 1959.

HILLER, LEJAREN A., and ISSACSON, LEONARD M. *Experimental Music*. New York: McGraw-Hill Book Co., 1959.

HINDEMITH, PAUL. *A Composer's World—Horizons and Limitations*. Cambridge, Mass.: Harvard University Press, 1952.

113

HOLST, IMOGEN. *Gustav Holst*. (With a note by Ralph Vaughan-Williams.) London: Oxford University Press, 1938.

HOOVER, KATHLEEN O'DONNELL, and CAGE, JOHN. *Virgil Thomson; His Life and Music*. New York: Thomas Yoseloff, 1959.

HOWARD, JOHN TASKER. *Our American Music*. Third edition. New York: Thomas Y. Crowell Co., 1939.

HOWES, FRANK STEWART. *The Music of William Walton*. Second edition. London: Oxford University Press, 1947.

JOHNSON, HAROLD E. *Jean Sibelius*. New York: Alfred A. Knopf, 1959.

KENNAN, KENT W. *Counterpoint; Based on 18th Century Practice*. Englewood Cliffs, N. J.: Prentice-Hall, 1959.

KOLODIN, IRVING. *The Composer As Listener; A Guide to Music*. New York: Horizon Press, 1958.

KOLODIN, IRVING. *The Musical Life*. New York: Alfred A. Knopf, 1958.

LANDON, HOWARD C. R., editor. *Joseph Haydn; Collected Correspondence and London Notebooks*. London: Barrie Books, 1959.

LANG, PAUL HENRY. *Music in Western Civilization*. New York: W. W. Norton & Co., 1941.

LEHMAN, LOTTIE. *My Many Lives*. Translated by Frances Holden. New York: Boosey & Hawkes, 1948.

MAISEL, EDWARD M. *Charles T. Griffes; The Life of an American Composer*. New York: Alfred A. Knopf, 1943.

MAREK, GEORGE R., editor. *The World Treasury of Grand Opera*. New York: Harper & Brothers, 1957.

MARTYNOV, IVAN I. *Dmitri Shostakovich, The Man and His Work*. Translated by T. Guralsky. New York: Philosophical Library, 1947.

MASON, DANIEL GREGORY. *The Quartets of Beethoven*. New York: Oxford University Press, 1947.

McKINNEY, HOWARD D., and ANDERSON, WILLIAM R. *Music in History; The Evolution of an Art*. New York: American Book Co., 1954.

MILHAUD, DARIUS. *Notes Without Music; An Autobiography*. Translated by Donald Evans. (Edited by Rollo Myers.) New York: Alfred A. Knopf, 1953.

MORGENSTERN, SAM, editor. *Composers on Music; An Anthology of Composers Writings from Palestrina to Copland*. New York: Pantheon Books, 1956.

MORRIS, REGINALD O. *Contrapuntal Technique in the 16th Century*. Oxford: Clarendon Press, 1922.

MUELLER, JOHN H. *The American Symphony Orchestra*. Bloomington: Indiana University Press, 1951.

114

NESTYEV, ISRAEL V. *Sergei Prokofiev, His Musical Life.* Translated by Rose Prokofieva. New York: Alfred A. Knopf, 1946.

NEWMAN, ERNEST. *More Essays from the World of Music.* New York: Coward-McCann, 1958.

NEWMAN, ERNEST. *More Stories of Great Operas.* Philadelphia: Blakiston Co., 1946.

NEWMAN, ERNEST. *Seventeen Famous Operas.* New York: Alfred A. Knopf, 1955.

NEWMAN, ERNEST. *Stories of Great Operas.* Philadelphia: Blakiston Co., 1945.

NEWMAN, ERNEST. *The Wagner Operas.* New York: Alfred Knopf, 1949.

NEWMAN, ERNEST. *Wagner as Man and Artist.* New York: Alfred A. Knopf, 1924.

NORMAN, GERTRUDE, and SHRIFTE, MIRIAM L., editors. *Letters of Composers; An Anthology.* New York: Alfred A. Knopf, 1946.

PINCHERLE, MARC. *Corelli; His Life, His Work.* Translated by Hubert E. M. Russell. New York: W. W. Norton & Co., 1956.

PRUNIERES, HENRY. *A New History of Music.* London: Macmillan & Co., Ltd., 1946.

READ, HERBERT. *Art and Society.* Revised edition. Toronto: Ryerson Press, 1945.

REESE, GUSTAVE. *Music in the Rennaissance.* New York: W. W. Norton & Co., 1954.

RIESEMANN, OSKAR VON. *Mussorgsky.* Translated by Paul England. New York: Alfred A. Knopf, 1929.

RIMSKY-KORSAKOV, NIKOLAI. *My Musical Life.* Translated from fifth revised edition by Judah A. Joffe. (Edited by Carl Van Vechten.) New York: Alfred A. Knopf, 1942.

ROLLAND, ROMAIN. *Essays on Music.* New York: Crown, 1948.

SACHS, CURT. *The Rise of Music in the Ancient World, East and West.* New York: W. W. Norton & Co., 1943.

SALAZAR, A. *Music in Our Time.* New York: W. W. Norton & Co., 1946.

SCHENK, ERICH. *Mozart and His Times.* Translated and edited by Richard and Clara Winston. New York: Alfred A. Knopf, 1959.

SEAMAN, JULIAN, editor. *Great Orchestral Music; A Treasury of Program Notes.* New York: Rinehart & Co., 1950.

SERAFF, VICTOR I. *Dmitri Shostakovich; The Life and Background of a Soviet Composer.* (In collaboration with Nodejda Galli-Shohot.) New York: Alfred A. Knopf, 1943.

SESSIONS, ROGER. *The Musical Experience of Composer, Performer, Listener.* Princeton, N. J.: Princeton University Press, 1950.

SHAW, GEORGE B. *The Perfect Wagnerite.* New York: Brentano, 1916.

SITWELL, SACHEVERELL. *Liszt.* Revised edition. New York: Philosophical Library, 1955.

SLONIMSKY, NICOLAS. *Lexicon of Musical Invective.* New York: Coleman-Ross, 1953.

STEFAN, PAUL. *Arturo Toscanini.* New York: Viking Press, 1936.

STEIN, JACK M. *Richard Wagner and the Synthesis of the Arts.* Detroit: Wayne University Press, 1960.

STODDARD, HOPE. *Symphony Conductors of the U. S. A.* New York: Thomas Y. Crowell Co., 1957.

STRAVINSKY, IGOR, and CRAFT, ROBERT EDUARD. *Conversations with Igor Stravinsky.* Garden City, L. I.: Doubleday & Co., 1959.

STRAVINSKY, IGOR. *Poetics of Music.* Translated by Arthur Knodel and Ingolf Dahl. Cambridge, Mass.: Harvard University Press, 1947.

TAUBMAN, HYMAN H. *The Maestro, The Life of Arturo Toscanini.* New York: Simon & Schuster, 1951.

TAYLOR, DEEMS. *Some Enchanted Evenings; The Story of Rodgers and Hammerstein.* New York: Harper & Brothers, 1953.

THOMPSON, OSCAR. *Practical Music Criticism.* New York: M. Witmark & Sons, 1934.

THOMSON, VIRGIL. *Music Right and Left.* New York: Henry Holt & Co., 1951.

TOCH, ERNST. *The Shaping Forces of Music.* New York: Criterion Music Corporation, 1948.

TOVEY, DONALD FRANCIS. *Essays in Musical Analysis.* Vol. 1, Symphonies; Vol. 2, Symphonies; Vol. 3, Concertos; Vol. 4, Illustrative Music—1956 edition; Vol. 5, Vocal Music—1956 edition; Vol. 6, Miscellaneous Notes—1957 edition. New York: Oxford University Press.

TOVEY, DONALD FRANCIS. *The Main Stream of Music and Other Essays.* New York: Oxford University Press, 1949.

ULRICH, HOMER. *Chamber Music: The Growth and Practice of an Intimate Art.* New York: Columbia University Press, 1948.

VARLEY, DOUGHLAS H. *African Native Music.* London: Royal Empire Society, 1936.

VAUGHAN-WILLIAMS, RALPH, and HOLST, GUSTAV. *Heirs and Rebels.* (Edited by Ursula Vaughan-Williams and Imogen Holst.) New York: Oxford University Press, 1959.

VAUGHAN-WILLIAMS, RALPH. *National Music.* New York: Oxford University Press, 1934.

VERDI, GIUSEPPE. *Verdi, The Man in His Letters: As Edited and Selected by Franz Werfel and Paul Stefan.* Translated by Edward Downes. New York: L. B. Fischer, 1942.

WEINSTOCK, HERBERT. *Handel.* Second revised edition. New York: Alfred A. Knopf, 1959.

116

WHITE, ERIC W. *Benjamin Britten.* New York: Boosey and Hawkes, 1948.

YOUNG, PERCY M. *Tragic Muse: The Life and Works of Robert Schumann.* London: Hutchinson & Co., Ltd., 1957.

ZOFF, OTTO, editor. *Great Composers Through the Eyes of Their Contemporaries.* New York: E. P. Dutton & Co., 1951.

Literature and Music

SHIPLEY, JOSEPH T. *The Quest for Literature.* New York: Richard R. Smith, 1931.

Music Education and the Education of the Academically Talented and Gifted

ABRAHAM, WILLARD. *Common Sense About Gifted Children.* New York: Harper & Brothers, 1958.

BERNER, JEANNETTE C. *Educating Superior Students.* New York: American Book Co., 1935.

COHEN, HELEN LOUISE, and CORYELL, NANCY G., editors. *Educating Superior Students.* New York: American Book Co., 1935.

CRUICKSHANK, WILLIAM M. *Education of Exceptional Children and Youth.* Englewood Cliffs, N. J.: Prentice-Hall, 1958.

DE HAAN, R. F., and HAVIGHURST, R. J. *Educating Gifted Children.* Chicago: University of Chicago Press, 1957.

EARHART, WILL. *The Meaning and Teaching of Music.* New York: Witmark Educational Publication, 1935.

FRENCH, JOSEPH L. *Educating the Gifted.* New York: Henry Holt & Co., 1959.

FULLAGAR, WILLIAM A.; LEWIS, HAL G.; and CUMBEE, CARROLL F. *Readings for Educational Psychology.* New York: Thomas Y. Crowell Co., 1956.

GOODENOUGH, FLORENCE L. *Exceptional Children.* New York: Appleton-Century-Crofts, 1956.

LOOMIS, GRACE I. *The Education of the Gifted Child with Implications for School Practice.* Eugene: University of Oregon, 1951.

MURSELL, JAMES L. *Music Education; Principals and Programs.* Morristown, N. J.: Silver Burdett Co., 1956.

NATIONAL SOCIETY FOR THE STUDY OF EDUCATION. *Basic Concepts in Music Education.* Fifty-Seventh Yearbook, Part 1. (Edited by Nelson B. Henry.) Chicago: University of Chicago Press, 1958.

NATIONAL SOCIETY FOR THE STUDY OF EDUCATION. *The Integration of Educational Experiences.* Fifty-Seventh Yearbook, Part II. (Edited by Nelson B. Henry.) Chicago: University of Chicago Press, 1958.

SUMPTION, MERLE R., and LUECKING, EVELYN M. *Education of the Gifted.* New York: Ronald Press Co., 1960.

117

Music History

ABRAHAM, G. E. H., editor. *Handel, A Symposium*. New York: Oxford University Press, 1954.

ANDERSON, EMILY. *The Letters of Mozart and His Family*. New York: Macmillan Co., 1938.

ANDERSON, MARIAN. *My Lord, What A Morning*. New York: Viking Press, 1956.

APEL, PAUL. *Music of the Americas, North and South*. New York: Vantage Press, 1958.

BARNES, WILLIAM H. *The Contemporary American Organ; Its Evolution, Design, and Construction*. Glen Rock, N. J.: J. Fischer & Brother, 1930.

BARTOS, FRANTISEK. *Bedrich Smetana; Letters and Reminiscences*. Translated by Daphne Rusbidge. Prague: Artia, 1955.

BARZUN, JACQUES. *Berlioz and His Century*. Revised edition. New York: Meridian Books, 1956.

BEECHAM, SIR THOMAS. *Frederick Delius*. London: Hutchinson & Co., 1959.

BEETHOVEN, LUDWIG VAN. *New Beethoven Letters*. Translated and annotated by MacArdle and Ludwig Misch. Norman: University of Oklahoma Press, 1957.

BERGER, ARTHUR V. *Aaron Copland*. New York: Oxford University Press, 1953.

BERTENSSON, SERGEI, and LEYDY, JAY. *Sergei Rachmaninoff; A Lifetime in Music*. New York: New York University Press, 1956.

BIANCOLLI, LOUIS L. *The Mozart Handbook; A Guide to the Man and His Music*. Cleveland: World Publishing Co., 1954.

BONAVIA, FERRUCCIO. *Verdi*. London: Dennis Dobson, Ltd., 1947.

BRAHMS, JOHANNES, and BILLRATH, THEODORE. *Letters from a Musical Friendship*. Translated and edited by Hans Barkan. Norman: University of Oklahoma Press, 1957.

BRAHMS, JOHANNES, and SCHUMANN, CLARA. *Letters of Clara Schumann and Johannes Brahms*. (Edited by Litzmann.) New York: Longmans, Green & Co., 1927.

BRION, MARCEL. *Schumann and the Romantic Age*. Translated by Geoffrey Sainsbury. New York: Macmillan Co., 1956.

BRODER, NATHAN. *Samuel Barber*. New York: Schirmer, 1954.

BROWN, MAURICE J. *Schubert; A Critical Biography*. London: Macmillan & Co., Ltd., 1958.

BUKOFZER, MANFRED F. *Studies in Medieval and Renaissance Music*. New York: W. W. Norton & Co., 1950.

BURK, JOHN N. *Mozart and His Music*. New York: Random House, 1959.

BURK, JOHN N. *The Life and Works of Beethoven*. New York: Random House, 1943.

BUSONI, FERRUCCIO B. *The Essence of Music and Other Papers.* Translated by Rosamond Ley. New York: Philosophical Library, 1957.

CALVOCORESSI, MICHEL D. *Modest Mussorgsky, His Life and Works.* (Edited by Gerald Abraham.) London: Rockliff, 1956.

CALVOCORESSI, MICHEL D. *Mussorgsky.* New York: E. P. Dutton & Co., 1946.

CANNON, BEEKMAN C.; JOHNSON, ALVIN H.; and WAITE, WILLIAM G. *The Art of Music, A Short History of Musical Styles and Ideas.* New York: Thomas Y. Crowell Co., 1960.

CAPELL, RICHARD. *Schubert's Songs.* Second edition. New York: Macmillan Co., 1957.

CARNER, MOSCO. *Puccini; A Critical Biography.* New York: Alfred A. Knopf, 1958.

CHAMBERS, GEORGE BENNET. *Folksong, Plainsong; A Study in Origins and Musical Relationships.* London: Merlin Press, 1956.

CHASINS, ABRAM. *The Van Cliburn Legend.* Garden City, L. I.: Doubleday & Co., 1959.

CHOTZINOFF, SAMUEL. *Toscanini, An Intimate Portrait.* New York: Alfred A. Knopf, 1956.

CORREDOR, JOSE MARIA. *Conversations with Casals.* Translated by André Mangeot. New York: E. P. Dutton & Co., 1956.

CORTOT, ALFRED. *In Search of Chopin.* Translated by Cyril and Rena Clarke. London: Peter Nevill, Ltd., 1951.

COWELL, HENRY, and COWELL, SIDNEY. *Charles Ives and His Music.* New York: Oxford University Press, 1955.

DEUTSCH, OTTO E. *Schubert; Memoirs by His Friends.* Translated by Rosamond Ley and John Nowell. New York: Macmillan Co., 1958.

D'INDY, VINCENT. *Beethoven: A Critical Biography.* Translated by Theodore Baker. New York: Schirmer, 1940.

EINSTEIN, ALFRED. *Mozart, His Character, His Work.* Translated by Arthur Mendel and Nathan Broder. New York: Oxford University Press, 1945.

EINSTEIN, ALFRED. *Schubert; A Musical Portrait.* New York: Oxford University Press, 1951.

EKMAN, KARL. *Jan Sibelius; His Life and Personality.* New York: Alfred A. Knopf, 1938.

FARMER, HENRY G. *Military Music.* New York: Chanticleer Press, 1950.

FENBY, ERIC. *Delius As I Knew Him.* London: G. Bell & Sons, Ltd., 1937.

FISCHLER, HANS. *The Perceptive Music Listener.* Englewood Cliffs, N. J.: Prentice-Hall, 1955.

FLEMING, WILLIAM, and VEINUS, ABRAHAM. *Understanding Music; Style, Structure, and History.* New York: Henry Holt & Co., 1958.

Foss, Hubert. *Ralph Vaughan-Williams; A Study.* New York: Oxford University Press, 1950.

Furtwangler, Wilhelm. *Concerning Music.* New York: Boosey & Hawkes, 1953.

Garfias, Robert. *Gagaku, The Music and Dances of the Japanese Imperial Household.* (Edited by Lincoln Kirstein.) New York: Theatre Arts Books, 1959.

Geiringer, Karl. *Brahms, His Life and Work.* Second edition. New York: Oxford University Press, 1947.

Geiringer, Karl. *Haydn, A Creative Life in Music.* New York: W. W. Norton & Co., 1946.

Geiringer, Karl. *The Bach Family; Seven Generations of Creative Genius.* New York: Oxford University Press, 1954.

Gilman, Lawrence. *Orchestral Music: An Armchair Guide.* (Edited by Edward Cushing.) New York: Oxford University Press, 1951.

Gilman, Lawrence. *Toscanini and Great Music.* New York: Farrar and Rinehart, 1938.

Grant, Margaret, and Hettinger, Herman S. *America's Symphony Orchestras and How They Are Supported.* New York: W. W. Norton & Co., 1940.

Green, Abel, and Laurie, Joe. *Show Biz.* New York: Garden City Books, 1952.

Hall, James H. *The Art Song.* Norman: University of Oklahoma Press, 1953.

Hanson, Howard. *Music in Contemporary American Civilization.* Lincoln: University of Nebraska Press, 1951.

Hart, Moss. *Act One.* New York: Random House, 1959.

Hartog, Howard. *European Music in the 20th Century.* London: Routledge & Kegan Paul, Ltd., 1957.

Herzog, George. *Research in Primitive and Folk Music in the United States, A Survey.* Washington, D. C.: Executive Offices, American Council of Learned Societies, 1936.

Heseltine, Philip. *Frederick Delius.* Revised edition. London: Bodley Head, 1952.

Hindemith, Paul. *Johann Sebastian Bach; Heritage and Obligation.* New Haven: Yale University Press, 1952.

Holst, Imogen. *The Music of Gustav Holst.* New York: Oxford University Press, 1951.

Howard, John Tasker, and Bellows, George K. *A Short History of Music in America.* New York: Thomas Y. Crowell Co., 1957.

Howe, Mark Antony DeWolfe. *The Tale of Tanglewood.* New York: Vanguard Press, 1946.

Howes, Frank. *The Music of Ralph Vaughan-Williams.* New York: Oxford University Press, 1954.

120

JACKSON, GEORGE PULLEN. *The Story of the Sacred Harp—1844-1944.* Nashville: Vanderbilt University Press, 1944.

JACOB, GORDON. *How To Read a Score.* New York: Boosey & Hawkes, 1944.

JACOB, H. E. *Joseph Haydn; His Art, Times and Glory.* New York: Rinehart & Co., 1950.

JOHNSON, HARRIETT. *Your Career in Music.* New York: E. P. Dutton & Co., 1944.

JONES, A. *Studies in African Music.* London: Oxford University Press, 1959.

KENYON, MAX. *A Mozart Letter Book.* Westport, Conn.: Associated Booksellers, 1956.

KOLODIN, IRVING. *The Story of the Metropolitan Opera—1883-1950.* New York: Alfred A. Knopf, 1953.

KRUEGER, KARL. *The Way of the Conductor; His Origins, Purposes and Procedures.* New York: Charles Scribner's Sons, 1958.

LAPRADE, ERNEST. *Broadcasting Music.* New York: Rinehart & Co., 1947.

LAWLESS, RAY MCKINLEY. *Folksingers and Folksongs in America.* New York: Duell, Sloan & Pearce, 1960.

LEIBOWITZ, RENE. *Schoenberg and His School.* Translated by Dika Newlin. New York: Philosophical Library, 1949.

LEICHTENTRITT, HUGO. *Music, History, and Ideas.* Cambridge, Mass.: Harvard University Press, 1938.

LEICHTENTRITT, HUGO. *Music of the Western Nations.* (Edited and amplified by Nicolas Slonimsky.) Cambridge, Mass.: Harvard University Press, 1956.

LEONHARD, CHARLES. *Recreation Through Music.* New York: A. S. Barnes & Co., 1952.

LOCKSPEISER, E., editor. *Debussy.* New York: Pellegrini & Cudahy, 1952.

LOWERY, HARRY. *A Guide to Musical Acoustics.* London: Dennis Dobson, Ltd., 1956.

LUPER, ALBERT T. *The Music of Brazil.* Washington, D. C.: Music Division, Pan-American Union, 1943.

MACHLIS, JOSEPH. *The Enjoyment of Music.* New York: W. W. Norton & Co., 1957.

McKINNEY, HOWARD D. *Music and Man.* New York: American Book Co., 1953.

MAHLER, ALMA. *Gustav Mahler—Memories and Letters.* New York: Viking Press, 1946.

MALM, WILLIAM P. *Japanese Music and Musical Instruments.* Rutland, Vt.: Charles E. Tuttle Co., 1959.

MANN, ALFRED. *The Study of Fugue.* New Brunswick, N. J.: Rutgers University Press, 1958.

MATTFELD, JULIUS. *Variety Music Cavalcade—1620-1950.* New York: Prentice-Hall, 1952.

MEYER, HAZEL. *The Gold in Tin Pan Alley.* Philadelphia: J. B. Lippincott Co., 1958.

MEYER, LEONARD B. *Emotion and Meaning in Music.* Chicago: University of Chicago Press, 1956.

MOORE, DOUGLAS S. *From Madrigal to Modern Music; A Guide to Musical Styles.* New York: W. W. Norton & Co., 1942.

NEWLIN, DIKA. *Bruckner, Mahler, Schoenberg.* New York: King's Crown Press, 1947.

NEWMAN, ERNEST. *From the World of Music.* (Essays from the Sunday Times selected by Felix Aprahanian.) London: John Calder, Ltd., 1956.

NEWMAN, ERNEST, editor. *Memoirs of Hector Berlioz.* New York: Tudor Publishing Co., 1947.

NEWMARCH, ROSA. *Jean Sibelius.* Boston: C. C. Birchard Co., 1939.

OLDROYD, GEORGE. *The Technique and Spirit of Fugue.* New York: Oxford University Press, 1948.

PARMET, SIMON. *The Symphonies of Sibelius.* Translated by Kingsley A. Hart. London: Cassell & Co., Ltd., 1959.

PINCHERLE, MARC. *An Illustrated History of Music.* Translated by Rollo Myers. (Edited by Georges and Rosamond Bernier.) New York: Reynal & Hitchcock, 1959.

PISTON, WALTER. *Harmony.* Revised edition. New York: W. W. Norton & Co., 1948.

REDLICH, HANS F. *Alban Berg, The Man and His Music.* London: John Calder, Ltd., 1957.

REDLICH, HANS F. *Bruckner and Mahler.* New York: Farrar, Straus and Cudahy, 1955.

RETI, RUDOLPH R. *Tonality, Atonality, Pantonality; A Study of Some Trends in 20th Century Music.* New York: Macmillan Co., 1958.

RIESEMANN, OSKAR VON. *Rachmaninoff Recollections.* New York: Macmillan Co., 1934.

RONGA, LUIGI. *The Meeting of Poetry and Music.* Translated by Elio Gianturco and Clara Rosanti. New York: Merlin Press, 1956.

SACHS, CURT. *Our Musical Heritage; A Short History of Music.* Second edition. New York: Prentice-Hall, 1955.

SACHS, CURT. *Rhythm and Tempo; A Study in Music History.* New York: W. W. Norton & Co., 1953.

SARGEANT, WINTHROP. *Listening to Music; With Drawings by Laszlo.* New York: Dodd, Mead & Co., 1958.

SCHOENBERG, ARNOLD. *Style and Idea.* New York: Philosophical Library, 1950.

SCHRADE, LEO. *Monteverdi: Creator of Modern Music.* New York: W. W. Norton & Co., 1950.

122

SCHREIBER, FLORA R., and PERISCHETTI, VINCENT. *William Schuman.* New York: Schirmer, 1954.

SCHUMANN, ELISABETH. *German Song.* Translated by D. Millar Craig. New York: Chanticleer Press, 1948.

SCHWEITZER, ALBERT. *J. S. Bach.* (2 vols.) Translated by Ernest Newman. New York: Macmillan Co., 1950.

SEROFF, VICTOR I. *Debussy, Musician of France.* New York: G. P. Putnam's Sons, 1956.

SEROFF, VICTOR I. *Maurice Ravel.* New York: Henry Holt & Co., 1953.

SEROFF, VICTOR I. *The Mighty Five.* New York: Allen, Towne & Heath, 1956.

SESSIONS, ROGER. *Reflections on the Musical Life in the U.S.* New York: Merlin Press, 1956.

SHAW, GEORGE B. *Shaw on Music; A Selection from the Music Criticism of Bernard Shaw Made by Eric Bentley.* Garden City: L. I.: Doubleday & Co., 1955.

SKINNER, FRANK. *Underscore. How A Motion Picture Score is Written, Arranged, and Recorded.* New York: Criterion Music Corporation, 1960.

SMITH, CECIL M. *Worlds of Music.* Philadelphia: J. B. Lippincott Co., 1952.

SMITH, JULIA FRANCES. *Aaron Copland; His Work and Contribution to American Music.* New York: E. P. Dutton & Co., 1955.

SPITTA, PHILLIP. *Johann Sebastian Bach.* (2 vols.) Translated by Clara Bell and J. A. Fuller-Maitland. New York: Dover Publications, 1951.

STEFAN, PAUL. *Anton Dvorak.* New York: Greystone Press, 1941.

STEVENS, HALSEY. *The Life and Music of Béla Bartók.* New York: Oxford University Press, 1953.

STRAUSS, RICHARD. *Recollections and Reflections.* London: Boosey & Hawkes, Ltd., 1953.

THAYER, A. W. *The Life of Ludwig Van Beethoven.* (3 vols.) Revised by Henry Krehbiel. New York: The Beethoven Association, 1921.

THOMPSON, HELEN M. *The Community Symphony Orchestra; How to Organize and Develop It.* Charleston, W. Va.: American Symphony Orchestra League, 1952.

THOMPSON, OSCAR. *Debussy, Man and Artist.* New York: Dodd, Mead & Co., 1937.

THOMSON, VIRGIL. *The Art of Judging Music.* New York: Alfred A. Knopf, 1948.

THOMSON, VIRGIL. *The Musical Scene.* New York: Alfred A. Knopf, 1945.

THURMAN, HOWARD. *Deep River; An Interpretation of Negro Spirituals.* Mills College, Calif.: The Eucalyptus Press, 1945.

123

Tovey, Donald Francis. *A Musician Talks*. New York: Oxford University Press, 1941.

Tovey, Donald Francis. *Beethoven*. London: Oxford University Press, 1945.

Tovey, Donald Francis. *The Forms of Music*. New York: Meridian Books, 1956.

Ulrich, Homer. *Music; A Design for Listening*. New York: Harcourt, Brace & Co., 1956.

Ulrich, Homer. *Symphonic Music; Its Evolution Since the Renaissance*. New York: Columbia University Press, 1952.

Vallas, Leon. *César Franck*. Translated by Hubert Foss. New York: Oxford University Press, 1951.

Vallas, Leon. *Claude Debussy, His Life and Works*. Translated by Maire and Grace O'Brien. London: Oxford University Press, 1933.

Vaughan-Williams, Ralph. *The Making of Music*. Ithaca, N. Y.: Cornell University Press, 1955.

Walter, Bruno. *Gustav Mahler*. New York: Greystone Press, 1941.

Walter, Bruno. *Theme and Variations*. Translated by James Galston. New York: Alfred A. Knopf, 1946.

Weinstock, Herbert. *Chopin: The Man and His Music*. New York: Alfred A. Knopf, 1949.

Weinstock, Herbert. *Tchaikovsky*. New York: Alfred A. Knopf, 1943.

Wellesz, Egon. *The Origins of Schoenberg's Twelve-Tone System*. Washington, D. C.: U.S. Government Printing Office, 1958.

Werfel, Franz, and Stefan, Paul, editors. *Verdi, The Man in His Letters*. Translated by Edward Downes. New York: L. B. Fischer. 1942.

Ybarra, Thomas R. *Verdi; Miracle Man of Opera*. New York: Harcourt, Brace & Co., 1955.

The Orchestra

Bekker, Paul. *The Story of the Orchestra*. New York: W. W. Norton & Co., 1936.

Berlioz, Hector. *Evenings with the Orchestra*. Translated and edited by Jacques Barzun. New York: Alfred A. Knopf, 1956.

Berlioz, Hector. *Treatise on Instrumentation*. Translated by Theodore Front. Enlarged and revised by Richard Strauss. New York: Kalmus, 1948.

Forsyth, Cecil. *Orchestration*. New York: Macmillan Co., 1936.

Geiringer, Karl. *Musical Instruments*. New York: Oxford University Press, 1945.

Kennan, Kent. *The Technique of Orchestration*. Englewood Cliffs, N. J.: Prentice-Hall, 1952.

PISTON, WALTER. *Orchestration.* New York: W. W. Norton & Co., 1955.

RIMSKY-KORSAKOV, NIKOLAI. *Principles of Orchestration.* New York: Kalmus, 1922.

SACHS, CURT. *The History of Musical Instruments.* New York: W. W. Norton & Co., 1940.

FILMS

Concerts on Film. 26 min., 16mm, sound, b & w. Mills Picture Corporation, 6533 Hollywood Boulevard, Hollywood 28, California, 1954.

> A series of films of unsurpassed musical quality made by some of the world's greatest concert artists:
> Jascha Heifetz #103
> Jascha Heifetz #104
> Arthur Rubinstein #101
> Arthur Rubinstein #102
> Gregor Piatigorsky #105
> Trio—Heifetz, Rubinstein, Piatigorsky #107
> Marian Anderson #108

Hearing the Orchestra. 13 min., 16mm, sound, b. & w. McGraw-Hill Book Co., Text-film Department, 330 West 42nd Street, New York 18, New York, 1952.

Hymn of the Nations. 28 min., 16mm, sound, b. & w. Government Films Department, United World Films, 1445 Park Avenue, New York 29, New York, 1945.

> An indescribably superb film in which Arturo Toscanini conducts the NBC Symphony Orchestra in the music of Verdi, including "The Hymn of the Nations."

Instruments of the Orchestra. 20 min., 16mm, sound, b. & w. British Information Services, 30 Rockefeller Plaza, New York 20, New York, 1947.

> Benjamin Britten—Young Person's Guide to the Orchestra. Sir Malcolm Sargent and The London Symphony Orchestra. Instruments in small sections and in full orchestra. Explanations.

Music as a Language (13 films). 29 min. each, 16mm, sound, b & w. National Educational Television and Radio Center, 2320 Washtenaw Avenue, Ann Arbor, Michigan. 1955.

A series of 13 exceptionally superior films made by Dr. Howard Hanson of the Eastman School of Music at Rochester, New York:

Music and Emotion	Meter and Rhythm
Music as Sound	Narrative Music
The Alphabet in Black	The Romantic Symphony
The Alphabet in White	Merry Mount
Musical Words	Colors in Music
Modern Music	An Essay in Sound
Six Basic Categories	

Pablo Casals. 26 min., 16mm, sound, b & w. Mills Picture Corporation, 6533 Hollywood Boulevard, Hollywood 28, California, 1955.

Film portrait of the cellist, showing episodes in his daily life. Performance of "Suite No. 1 in G Major" by Bach in the ancient Abbey Church of St. Michel-de-Cuxa. Film takes place in Prades.

Pacific 231. 11 min., 16mm, sound, b & w. Young America Films, 18 East 41st Street, New York 17, New York, 1952.

Based on the composition by Honegger. Visualization of journey of locomotive Pacific 231 through French countryside. Without narration. Film is a visual interpretation of the music, played by a symphony orchestra and conducted by the composer.

PUBLICATIONS OF THE NEA PROJECT ON THE ACADEMICALLY TALENTED STUDENT

The Identification and Education of the Academically Talented Student in the American Secondary School—Conference Report_____$1.50

Mathematics for the Academically Talented Student _____ .60

Science for the Academically Talented Student__ .60

Administration—Procedures and School Practices for the Academically Talented Student_____ 1.25

English for the Academically Talented Student__ 1.00

Modern Foreign Languages and the Academically Talented Student _____ 1.00

Social Studies for the Academically Talented Student _____ 1.00

NATIONAL EDUCATION ASSOCIATION

Clarice Kline, President
William G. Carr, Executive Secretary
Lyle W. Ashby, Deputy Executive Secretary

MUSIC EDUCATORS NATIONAL CONFERENCE

Allen P. Britton, President
Vanett Lawler, Executive Secretary

**ACADEMICALLY TALENTED
STUDENT PROJECT**

Charles E. Bish, Director